Ancient Israel

An Enthralling Guide to Jewish Kingdoms and the Israelites

© Copyright 2023 - All rights reserved.

The content contained within this book may not be reproduced, duplicated, or transmitted without direct written permission from the author or the publisher.

Under no circumstances will any blame or legal responsibility be held against the publisher, or author, for any damages, reparation, or monetary loss due to the information contained within this book, either directly or indirectly.

Legal Notice:

This book is copyright protected. It is only for personal use. You cannot amend, distribute, sell, use, quote, or paraphrase any part, or the content within this book, without the consent of the author or publisher.

Disclaimer Notice:

Please note the information contained within this document is for educational and entertainment purposes only. All effort has been executed to present accurate, up-to-date, reliable, and complete information. No warranties of any kind are declared or implied. Readers acknowledge that the author is not engaging in the rendering of legal, financial, medical, or professional advice. The content within this book has been derived from various sources. Please consult a licensed professional before attempting any techniques outlined in this book.

By reading this document, the reader agrees that under no circumstances is the author responsible for any losses, direct or indirect, that are incurred as a result of the use of the information contained within this document, including, but not limited to, errors, omissions, or inaccuracies.

Free limited time bonus

Stop for a moment. We have a free bonus set up for you. The problem is this: we forget 90% of everything that we read after 7 days. Crazy fact, right? Here's the solution: we've created a printable, 1-page pdf summary for this book that you're reading now. All you have to do to get your free pdf summary is to go to the following website:

https://livetolearn.lpages.co/enthrallinghistory/

Once you do, it will be intuitive. Enjoy, and thank you!

Table of Contents

INTRODUCTION 1
CHAPTER 1: WHO WERE THE ANCIENT ISRAELITES? 4
CHAPTER 2: HENOTHEISM AND YAHWISM 10
CHAPTER 3: THE IRON AGE 18
CHAPTER 4: BIBLICAL REFERENCES TO ANCIENT ISRAEL 28
CHAPTER 5: THE KINGDOM OF JUDAH 39
CHAPTER 6: THE PERSIAN PERIOD 48
CHAPTER 7: THE HELLENISTIC PERIOD (330-50 BCE) 58
CHAPTER 8: THE HASMONEAN DYNASTY (140-37 BCE) 67
CHAPTER 9: THE HERODIAN DYNASTY (37 BCE-100 CE) 80
CONCLUSION 94
HERE'S ANOTHER BOOK BY ENTHRALLING HISTORY THAT YOU MIGHT LIKE 96
FREE LIMITED TIME BONUS..97
BIBLIOGRAPHY 98

Introduction

The history of ancient Israel is a fascinating subject that has intrigued scholars, theologians, and enthusiasts for centuries. Israel was a small but influential state located in the eastern Mediterranean region that existed from around 1200 BCE until its destruction by the Babylonian Empire in 586 BCE. It continued to exist under the rule of various empires, including the Persians, the Greeks, and the Romans. The region and its people boast a rich and interesting history that is marked by great religious significance, which continues to influence present-day society and the world.

Beginning in the Bronze Age, the region occupied by the Israelites boasted a more diverse ethnic identity since it was occupied by various peoples and tribes. The story of the Israelites did not begin until the Iron Age when they began to emerge as distinct people with an identifiable culture, tradition, and identity. They began to form their own kingdom, which occurred with the movement of the Israelites from Sinai to Canaan, where they established their own rule under King Saul, though it was Joshua who led the Israelites to the land promised to them by Yahweh.

The period that immediately followed was filled with great prosperity for the Israelites. Under King Solomon, the region was able to extend its influence beyond its borders, becoming a center of culture, trade, and religious learning. However, following the death of Solomon, the kingdom split into two: the Kingdom of Israel in the north and the Kingdom of Judah in the south. While both these regions would eventually fall to foreign invaders, they did much damage to themselves through persistent internecine conflicts.

Despite its relatively short existence, ancient Israel has left an indelible mark on world history. The biblical traditions and stories that emerged from this period have influenced not only Judaism but also Christianity and Islam and have had a significant impact on Western culture and civilization. The story of ancient Israel is of great interest to historians and archaeologists, who have been studying the region and its people for many decades.

Perhaps most significantly, the Israelites created a monotheistic religion, which was unheard of in the ancient Near East besides Zoroastrianism (some debate whether this religion fits the definition of a monotheistic religion, though). Most religions practiced at the time were polytheistic, so the worship of a single god challenged a widely accepted worldview. The Hebrew Bible, also known as the Old Testament, is a collection of sacred texts that tells the story of the Israelites and their relationship with God. These texts contain historical accounts, poetry, wisdom, and prophetic writings that have inspired generations of believers.

Archaeologists have long attempted to establish historical evidence for the story narrated in the Bible. The study of ancient Israel is also important for understanding the broader history of the eastern Mediterranean region. The Israelites were part of a larger cultural and economic network that included the Phoenicians, the Assyrians, the Babylonians, and the Persians. The region was a crossroads of trade and cultural exchange, and its history is characterized by a series of conquests, migrations, and interactions between different groups.

This book on ancient Israel aims to provide a comprehensive overview of the history, culture, and religion of this fascinating period. It explores the major events, personalities, and themes that shaped ancient Israel and its legacy. It also examines the historical and archaeological evidence that has been uncovered in recent years, shedding new light on the lives and beliefs of the Israelites.

Offering a comprehensive overview of the religious history of the Israelites, this book follows their journey through the Iron Age, when the people first began to gain an identity of their own. It continues through to the Babylonian exile, when the Israelites were forced out of their homes, to the Persian period, when they were liberated. The emergence of the Greeks in the region is also discussed, as well as the religious role and significance of the Israelites. The final topic of the book is the Herodian dynasty and its fall to the Romans, marking the end of the Israelite region as it was then known.

Chapter 1: Who Were the Ancient Israelites?

Between the 12th and 6th centuries BCE, the Near East region was occupied by a group of people known as the Israelites. This Semitic-speaking group of twelve tribes was believed to be the descendants of Abraham, moving from Mesopotamia to Canaan around the 2nd millennium BCE. As such, their culture, religion, and way of life are believed to have emerged from the Canaanite tradition, although they would go on to develop their own distinct ethnic and cultural identity.

At the time, Canaan was a culturally diverse region populated by various tribes. These included the Canaanites, the Jebusites, and the Philistines. The first recorded mention of the Israelites comes from an unlikely account of an Egyptian victory over the Libyans during the reign of Pharaoh Merneptah. This mention appears misplaced, as it makes them seem as if they were an established political power rather than a nomadic people. This has led to the speculation that the Israelites might have been part of the Libyan coalition.

The Religious History of the Israelites

The Israelites held great religious significance, as they believed themselves to be the chosen people of God. Although there are extra-biblical mentions of the Israelites, historians still rely on biblical accounts to help navigate the history of the ancient Israelites. The biblical accounts narrate the ancestry of the Israelites, who descended from Abraham. He followed God's command to leave his homeland of Ur and move to Canaan. The religious history and journey of the Israelites can be found in the Hebrew Bible. However, since historical facts mix with legends and religious teachings, it can be hard to determine the sequence of events.

Between the 10th and 7th centuries, the Israelites practiced a religion that was considered largely polytheistic in nature. It was actually closer to henotheism, meaning that while they worshiped several deities, their primary worship revolved around a single god. Yahweh was the primary deity of worship for the Judeans and the Israelites.

The Israelites performed acts of worship in temples and synagogues and observed animal sacrificial rituals, which were a central aspect of tribal life. Canaan was believed to be the homeland God had appointed for the Israelites, marking their special position in his eyes and enforcing a duty of subservience and worship on them.

History from the Bible

The biblical narrative found in the Torah traces the Israelites' origin to Jacob, whose family was forced to flee to Egypt because of a famine. After around four hundred years, Jacob's descendants had grown to include over 600,000 men, a number that alarmed the pharaoh of Egypt. As a precautionary measure against possible threats, he enslaved the Israelites and ordered any newborn son to be killed at birth.

A woman from the tribe of Levi hid her son and sent him down the Nile in a basket, where he was rescued by an Egyptian woman, which some accounts narrate as the daughter of the pharaoh. As an adult, he fled to Midian after killing an Egyptian slave master who was beating an Israelite. At the age of eighty, this man, who was named Moses, was called on by Yahweh to go to Mount Sinai and was told to lead the people of Israel out of Egypt.

However, the pharaoh refused to free the Israelites. In response, Yahweh struck the Egyptians with a series of calamities, including plague and famine, which resulted in the pharaoh relenting and banishing the Israelites from Egypt. As they began their journey, which is typically referred to as the Exodus, the pharaoh changed his mind and had his armies follow the Israelites as they came to the Red Sea. There, Moses performed a miracle, parting the sea to allow his people to cross. The pharaoh's armies drowned.

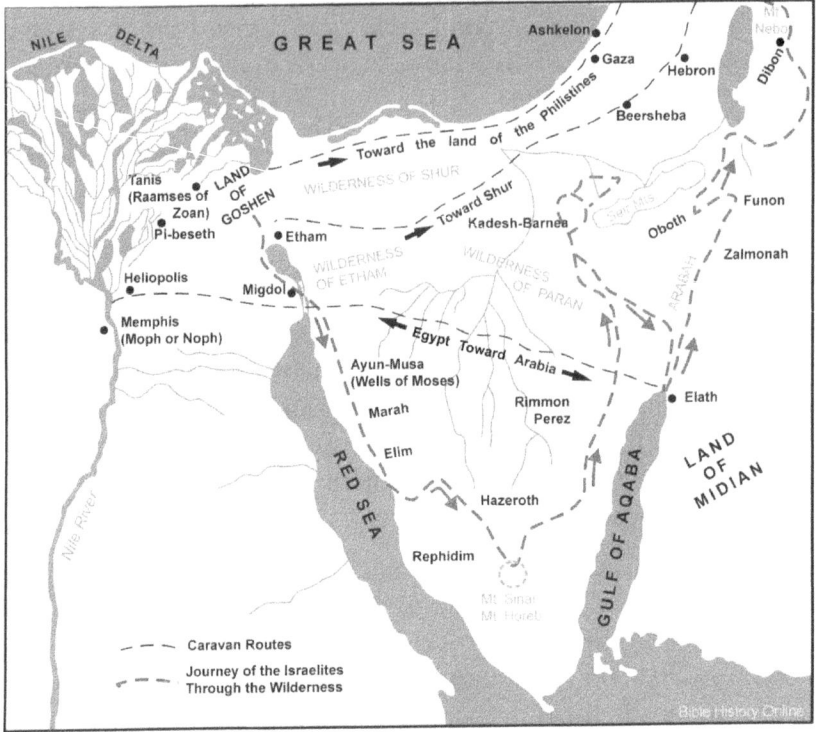

Israelites' Exodus from Egypt to Canaan.
https://bible-history.com/maps/route-exodus; Publication use is permitted with a link going to Bible History Online: https://bible-history.com/

The twelve tribes of Israel (Judah, Levi, Reuben, Simeon, Naphtali, Dan, Gad, Asher, Issachar, Zebulun, Joseph, and Benjamin) were then led to Mount Sinai, where Yahweh revealed the Ten Commandments, which Moses recorded along with the Torah. The twelve tribes agreed to be the chosen people of Yahweh and follow the Ten Commandments. However, they refused to march on and conquer the land of Canaan as ordered by Yahweh. As a result, the Israelites were condemned to exile and death in Sinai.

According to tradition, forty years later, a new generation led by Joshua entered Canaan and was allocated parts of this land. Yahweh appointed Saul king of the Israelites, followed by his son Eshbaal, who was then replaced by David. Under his and his son Solomon's rule, the Israelites established a monarchy and the First Temple of Jerusalem. Following Solomon's death, the kingdom was divided in two.

The tale that follows narrates the downfall of the two kingdoms. In the north, the Israelites forgot to worship God, instead permitting the worship of many deities. Thus, they lost Yahweh's favor. The Israelites were later conquered by foreigners and scattered across the lands. In the south, among the Judeans, some remained true to Yahweh, but some allowed the worship of other gods. They also fell to foreign rule, as they were taken into captivity by the Babylonians.

Yet they were not entirely forgotten. Their salvation came in the form of Cyrus the Great, the founder of the Achaemenid Empire. He conquered the Babylonians and allowed the Judeans to return to their homeland. Cyrus even helped them reconstruct their temple. However, the region remained part of the Persian Empire until the empire fell to Alexander the Great in 331 BCE.

Following the death of Alexander, the region was held by Ptolemy I, one of Alexander's generals. It was then held by the Seleucid Empire until the region was taken by Rome around 63 BCE. Unrest in the region continued, with the Jews revolting against suppression and foreign rule until the Bar Kokhba Revolt, which happened between the years 132 and 136. The Jews were defeated, and Jerusalem was renamed Syria Palaestina.

This is ancient Israelite history in a nutshell, but we will be exploring this history in more depth throughout the book. We will also provide historical evidence alongside the biblical narrative where applicable. But now that we have a basic idea of Israelite history, let's take a look at their traditions and the etymology of the name before diving further into the past.

Henotheism to Monotheism

The emergence of a monotheistic form of worship from henotheistic practices began with the Babylonian exile of the Israelites. During the exile, to maintain a sense of identity, the Israelites began to identify more with their religion, dedicating themselves more to living their lives in accordance with the Ten Commandments.

After the liberation of the Jews by the Persian Empire and their subsequent return to Jerusalem, they maintained this practice as a source of religious identity and unity that kept them together during captivity. Hence, Jewish practices abandoned the more henotheistic practices for a monotheistic form of worship.

Cultural Identity

The Israelite identity emerged from their religious history and dictated all aspects of life. For instance, knowledge and education were considered central to society. Much of it was based on the study and understanding of the Torah, which children were taught to read and write. Other than the sacred place it held as God's text, it also held great value as a gift of wisdom from God.

The legal system within Israelite society also stemmed from religion. The Ten Commandments were the rules by which a devout Hebrew or Israelite, as they were called following the conquest of Canaan, was to lead their life. The Torah provided an ethical framework that outlined just and fair behavior as members of society. These laws allowed for the protection of the weak and vulnerable and placed an emphasis on compassion and mercy.

Much of the Israelite experience was marked by oppression. While archaeological evidence does not support the idea that the Egyptians placed the Israelites in slavery, the Israelites faced subjugation throughout their history, with the region and the people being conquered by many different empires and rulers. They were often the subject of oppression because of their religious practice.

One of the most significant challenges faced by the Israelites was the Babylonian captivity when they were removed from their homes and forced into exile. Cyrus the Great's actions in freeing the Jews earned him a mention in the Bible.

The Etymology of the Word "Israelite"

The term "Israelite" is not of biblical origin but is first recorded among the inscriptions of Merneptah. The inscription itself talks about the destruction of "Israel." Since no such land existed at the time, the term is believed to have referred to a people group, perhaps the Israelite tribes that offered armed support to the Lydians in their conflict with Egypt.

In the biblical narrative, the name "Israel" was given to Jacob, who wrestled with God. The term comes from *yisra* ("to struggle with") and *el* ("god"). The Hebrew Bible uses the term "Israelites" to refer to the twelve tribes of Israel, and while this term is often used interchangeably with "Hebrew" and "Jew," this usage is not always appropriate. To be specific, the term "Israelites" refers to the immediate descendants of Jacob and those who converted to the faith. "Hebrews" refer to the descendants who lived in Canaan, and "Jews" refer to those emerging from the Israelite tribe of Judah and later formed the Kingdom of Judah.

While the monarchy lasted, the term "Israelite" was used to denote the people of that land and later to those belonging to Judah in light of the Babylonian exile of the Israelites. The term "Israel," which refers to the region and the ethnic group identified by their worship of Yahweh, emerged from the word "Israelite."

Archaeological efforts to find evidence confirming the movements of the Israelites, as narrated by the Bible, have turned up very little. The enslavement of the Israelites by the Egyptians, for example, is heavily discussed in the Bible but is not conclusively supported by archaeological evidence. The archaeological evidence suggests that the Israelites might have branched out into Canaan instead of taking the region by force, with their monotheistic religion slowly replacing the preexisting polytheism of Canaan.

Whatever may be the true facts, ancient Israelite history has had a profound impact on many aspects of society and religion in the present day. When the Israelites prospered, they gained great influence and saw success in the social and economic spheres. Beginning in the Iron Age, the Israelites began to emerge as a distinct people group in the Near East, and that is where we will start our next topic of discussion.

Chapter 2: Henotheism and Yahwism

Religious ideology and practice form an integral part of the way a society is organized. The understanding of ancient religious practice provides insight into the way regions were organized and the part religion played in people's lives.

Henotheism

Henotheistic worship emerged in Israelite thought between the 10th and 7th centuries BCE, slowly evolving from outright polytheism. Henotheism involves the worship of a single, supreme deity, but it does not preclude the existence and worship of other gods. While the worship of Yahweh was central to Israelite belief, it did not exclude the worship of other gods.

The term henotheism emerged from the works of Friedrich Schelling, who coined the German term *henotheismus*, meaning "one theism (god)." Henotheism often goes hand in hand with the concept of equitheism, the idea of the existence of multiple gods, all of whom are equal. Henotheistic belief is centered around the acceptance of the existence of numerous gods of equal divinity. However, there is one deity that reigns above all others and is the main focal point of the religion.

Since henotheism holds the worship of one god above others, many historians prefer the term monolatrism, a religion where one god is central without denying the existence or worship of other gods.

Henotheism may refer to the transitional period between polytheism and monotheism.

Greco-Roman Cultures

One example of henotheistic practices can be found in Greek and Roman cultures. Both cultures evolved from polytheistic beliefs to henotheistic worship. While the ancient Greek culture had many gods and deities, each of whom had distinct roles and personalities, different cities had patron gods that were held in higher esteem than others. The patron god for Athens was Athena, and Poseidon was the patron god of Corinth. The gods were all important, but most Greeks didn't worship the gods equally.

The supreme god did not always remain the same. In the case of Zeus, for example, Uranus acted as the supreme deity before him until he was overthrown by his son, Cronus. Zeus would overthrow Cronus, who had become tyrannical and swallowed his other children in an attempt to maintain supreme power. Zeus, the god of the sky and thunder, thus became the supreme deity of the Greeks.

While Roman culture was already structured based on a henotheistic setup, the assimilation of Greek facets during Rome's takeover of Greek in 146 BCE certainly helped it develop along the same lines. Roman gods held specialized duties, with Saturn being responsible for sowing and Ceres for the growth of grain. However, Jupiter helped supremacy over the other gods.

When the Romans entered Greek territory, and the two cultures began to mix, the Romans began to identify their gods with the Greek deities, and many Greek myths made their way into Roman culture and religious practice. The henotheistic way of life continued in the region until the arrival of Christianity.

Zoroastrianism

Zoroastrianism was the principal religion of the Achaemenid dynasty, as it was observed by the Persian rulers. While the religion was never imposed on Persian subjects, it is safe to assume that its existence and practice had some impact on them. The Zoroastrian religion held Ahura Mazda as the supreme god, but it did not disregard the presence of other deities.

Ahura Mazda was the being that signified goodness. He also had *yazatas* or good agents, such as Anahita and Mithra, which were responsible for providing for various aspects of life. They were held in high regard as well and were worshiped by the Persians in the pre-Islamic period.

Zoroastrian beliefs, which predate the emergence of Judaism, likely influenced Israelite beliefs in a number of ways. Most significantly, it can be seen in the concept of a struggle between good and evil and the concept of heaven and hell. In Zoroastrianism, the latter was a place of cleansing before meeting with the creator and was adopted as such in Judaism. Hell, as a place of eternal damnation, emerged later in Christian beliefs.

Hinduism

Hinduism offers one of the best examples of henotheism. Its scriptures, the Vedas, relate the worship of many gods, leading to the religion being seen as polytheistic in nature by many. However, despite the presence of many gods, one is held supreme, although a different section of the Vedas refers to different gods as being supreme, such as, for example, Agni, the god of fire, or Vac, the god of speech.

Similar to the Greek tradition, the Hindu gods underwent a power struggle, with the supreme god of the celestial waters, Varuna, being overthrown by Indra, who was supplanted by Vishnu and Shiva until they, too, were overthrown. The mixture of monotheism, monolatrism, polytheism, and even atheism within the Hindu tradition led to the appropriate classification of henotheism with an ever-evolving theistic framework.

Christianity

While Christianity is largely considered to be monotheistic, many of its characteristics, particularly among certain denominations, suggest that henotheism may be a more suitable categorization. Some religious experts attribute these categorizations to the Holy Trinity in Christian belief, which states God is the culmination of three equal beings with a single substance. Some early Christian groups made distinct differences in their worship, praising a supreme God and viewing Jesus as only an apparition of a perfect man.

Other Christian denominations, such as the Mormons, see three distinct beings where God rules supreme. The existence of other gods and goddesses is also implied in Mormon scripture, addressing a Heavenly "Mother" in addition to the "Heavenly Father." Despite this, Mormon worship revolves around one true God. Although the Church of Latter-day Saints does not consider itself henotheistic, some have suggested that the term may apply to them.

Some branches of Christianity also place a lot of importance on saints, praying to them instead of directly to God. Sometimes, these saints, such as Mother Mary, are attributed with supernatural powers, making them appear as deities, suggesting a henotheistic component.

Although people have made arguments that Christianity could be considered henotheistic in nature at times, it must be stressed that most people (even those outside of the religion) see it as being monotheistic.

Canaanite, Israelite, and Judean Beliefs

Many of the religions of the Iron Age were henotheistic in nature. In Canaanite practice, for example, the chief deities, El and Asherah, were believed to have seventy sons between them, all of whom ruled over regions of the earth and were, therefore, worshiped as gods.

The henotheistic nature of the Israelite tradition is a matter of contention since it was intended to be a monotheistic religion according to the Ten Commandments. However, evidence suggests the coexistence and worship of Yahweh and Asherah.

Religious beliefs from the Canaanite culture and the Israelite culture mixed to such an extent that the Canaanite god El became synonymous with Yahweh, leading some historians to believe they may have been the same god all along. Another factor that supports this theory is the existence of numerous remains of temples found in the Kingdom of Israel, including one altar depicting a bronze bull symbolizing Bull-El that predates the mention of Yahweh in the 12th century BCE.

The Israelite religion did not become truly monotheistic until the Babylonian captivity, when the Israelites began to strongly identify with their cultural heritage and create a separation between themselves and those around them.

Those who returned to Judah from the Babylonian exile were descendants of the people of Judah who had originally been exiled. As such, they had never lived in Judah prior to their return; however, they still considered themselves true Israelites. After securing positions of authority in Judah through Persian connections, the returnees began to institute their religion, which differed significantly from the principles of Yahwism. A new concept of priesthood began, a written scripture was produced, and written law became a primary focus. In a bid to protect their purity, the Judeans prohibited intercultural marriage.

Yahwism: The Ancient Israelite Religion

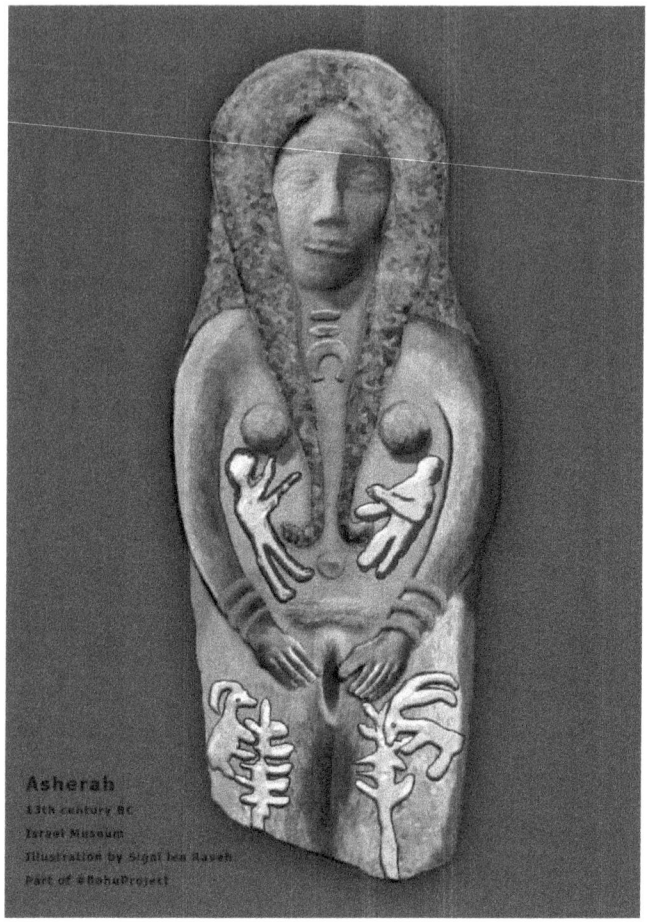

Asherah.
Sigal Lea Raveh, CC BY-SA 4.0 <https://creativecommons.org/licenses/by-sa/4.0>, via Wikimedia Commons; https://commons.wikimedia.org/wiki/File:Asherah_13th_century_BC_Israel_Museum.jpg

Considerable religious overlap can be seen when studying the religion of the ancient Israelites. Not only does the religion draw inspiration from earlier religions and those of surrounding regions, but it also underwent a metamorphosis itself, emerging from monotheistic underpinnings (the Ten Commandments) to a decidedly polytheistic and henotheistic framework. Religions, both new and old, had a great influence on the way Yahwism developed.

The term Yahwism stems from the worship of Yahweh, the central god of worship among the Kingdoms of Israel and Judah. While we know the history of the religion shows it as a monotheistic belief, with worship reserved only for Yahweh, the religion took on polytheistic themes. While Yahweh was the primary god worshiped by the Israelites, he was not the only one. He ruled alongside Asherah, the Canaanite goddess who was seen as the mother goddess. She was associated with sacred trees in the Canaanite and the Israelite religion. Indeed, in many places, the Canaanite goddess remained the supreme deity, followed by a cohort of secondary gods, each of whom had their own sets of prophets and devoted followers.

Yahwism involved many religious festivals, sacrifices, and rituals and played a role in resolving legal disputes. While some accounts suggest the Temple of Jerusalem was the sole temple for the worship of Yahweh, this was not the case; many others existed throughout the two kingdoms, with the king as the head of religion. His role was reflected in a ceremony, over which he presided, where Yahweh was enthroned in the Temple of Jerusalem.

As Yahwism evolved, it began to return to its monotheistic roots. This change occurred between the 10th century BCE and the 7th century BCE, becoming more widespread with the Babylonian exile when the ancient Israelites struggled to stay true to their roots and reject the influence of the surrounding culture. By the end of the 4th century BCE, Yahwism had evolved into Judaism and later led to the development and rise of Samaritanism, the largely monotheistic religion practiced by the Samaritans.

Beliefs of Yahwism

Yahwism is rarely categorized as monotheistic, with most historians seeing it as a polytheistic or henotheistic religion at best. Yahweh's temples also included statues of the goddess Asherah, indicating the high regard in which she was held. A series of second-tier gods and goddesses followed Yahweh and Asherah, such as Bal and Astarte, who had their own sets of priests.

Some accounts suggest that a third tier might also have existed, with this level of deities being specialist figures with specific and defined roles, such as Nehushtan, the god of snakebite cures. The fourth tier would have involved divine beings with a status slightly lower than that of gods. They acted as messengers to the deities. These beings would go on to be categorized as angels in Judaism, a distinct classification from a god.

Worship in Yahwism

Worship in the Yahwist tradition involved sacrifices, rituals, festivals, and vow-making, much like other Semitic religions. Existing largely as a rural region, Yahwist traditions coincided with major events that marked the Israelite way of life, which also later became entrenched into Israelite mythology, although their cultural relevance was not entirely lost. These were the events:

- *Passover*, with the birthing of the lambs, which was associated with the Exodus;
- *Shavuot*, with the cereal harvest season and the practice of implementing laws at Sinai;
- *Sukkot*, with the fruit harvest seasons and the wilderness wanderings when the Israelites were freed from slavery under the Egyptians.

In essence, these festivals were all intended to celebrate the blessings of Yahweh on the Israelites, their salvation, and their appointment as his chosen people. While prayer did not play a major role early on, sacrifices did. Before the Temple of Jerusalem had been destroyed, animal sacrifices were performed on its altar, and blood from the sacrifice was sprinkled around it. The sacrifices also became a symbol of atonement and purity but not until the end of the Babylonian exile when a monotheistic religious identity became more central to the Israelites.

The role of prophets and priests was extremely significant in the practice of Yahwism since they acted as messengers of Yahweh. Talismans and teraphims, small objects depicting deities, were noticeable components of worship among the Israelites, and worship itself was concentrated in high places like Mount Zion.

Yahwism's Evolution into Judaism

After the descendants of the exiled returned to Judah after the fall of Babylon, they found that life had continued while they had lived in suffering. While some accounts suggest that the exiled returned to Judah in vast numbers following the Persian conquest of Babylon, the truth is that only a small number returned home. While they had created their own identity in a foreign land, the returnees had no connection to Judah, having lived their whole lives in Babylon.

Those who had been exiled included the Judean elite, and their Persian connections helped them establish their version of society and religion. The religion of the returnees might not have been entirely monotheistic, but it would later take on such characteristics once Judaism was developed and the Torah became more widely accepted.

Chapter 3: The Iron Age

Natural disasters like earthquakes and droughts toward the end of the Bronze Age spurred mass migrations, pushing people to seek more sustainable lands. More significantly, the introduction of a new metal, iron, led to significant changes in the organization of life. Warfare changed, and the Bronze Age ended with the beginning of the Iron Age around 1200 BCE.

The end of the Bronze Age also marked the collapse of many civilizations, leading to the movement of nomadic tribes toward the mountainous regions along both sides of the Jordan River in Canaan. Around this time, the Sea Peoples invaded many countries along the Mediterranean, which is mentioned in Egyptian tablets. These tablets also referred to the Israelites.

Israelite Settlements

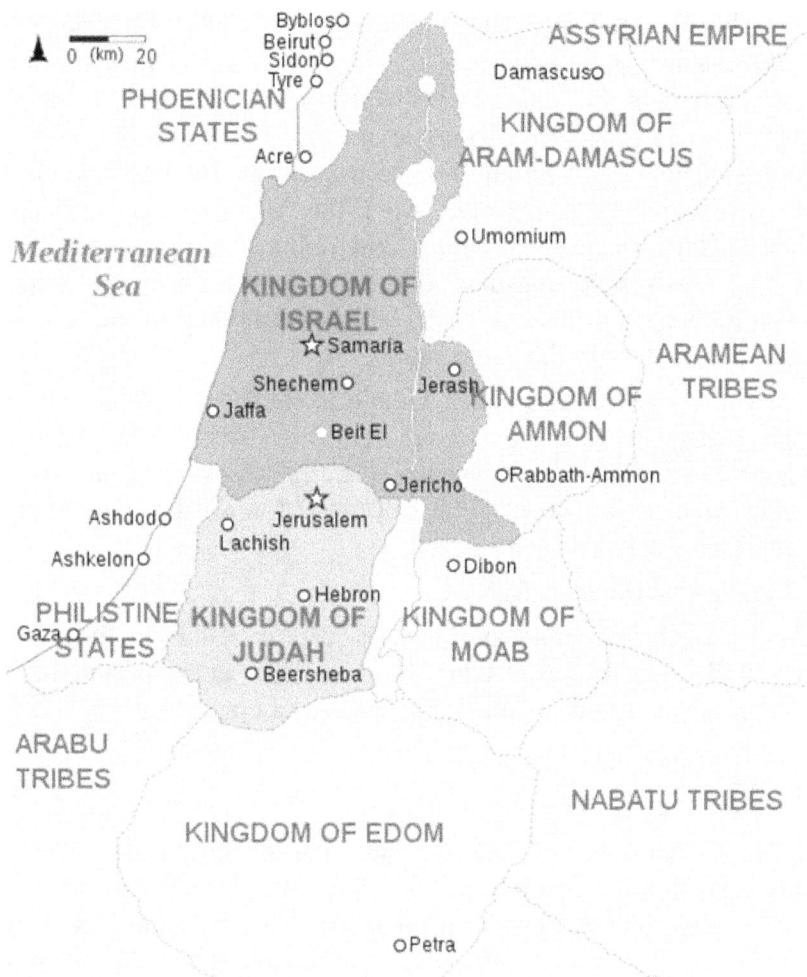

Iron Age settlements in the Kingdom of Israel and the Kingdom of Judah.
Oldtidens_Israel_&_Judea.svg: Finn WikiNoderivative work: Richardprins, CC BY-SA 3.0 <https://creativecommons.org/licenses/by-sa/3.0>, via Wikimedia Commons; https://commons.wikimedia.org/wiki/File:Kingdoms_of_Israel_and_Judah_map_830.svg

Early nomadic settlements in the region existed more as temporary encampments than permanent housing and consisted of a series of stone houses surrounding a yard-like space where livestock was kept. As the settlements grew and evolved, occupying greater spaces and needing more resources, they moved toward establishing more permanent housing. Archaeological evidence from these sites shows sheep and goat remains, as well as more cattle bones the longer the settlement occupied the region. Israelite settlements also had a noticeable absence of pig bones, reflecting the formation of their separate religious identity.

In the beginning, as the tribes migrated to Canaan, they numbered just about forty-five thousand people based on archaeological evidence, a far cry from the number of people during the establishment of the Kingdoms of Israel and Judah. The Iron Age saw the development and evolution of settlements, especially when the city of Shiloh (modern-day Khirbet Seilun) became a religious and political hub for the Israelite tribes. Their growing economic, political, social, and religious influence led to an independent Israelite state, which culminated in the formation of a unified kingdom under King Saul.

Before the establishment of a kingdom, the twelve tribes settled in separate groups in their allotted lands. When they felt threatened by neighboring civilizations, in particular, the Philistines, the tribes realized the need for a unified front. The call arose for a ruler, and Saul was appointed king of Israel.

A Timeline of the Iron Age

The Iron Age extends from the 12th century BCE to the early 6th century BCE. The phase did not progress as a single period but has instead been split into two distinct chronological eras.

- Iron Age I: 1200–950 BCE
- Iron Age II: 950–586 BCE

The first period of the Iron Age was marked by the decline of the Canaanite civilization as it had previously existed, a shift spurred by the end of the Bronze Age. The movements of new civilizations and tribes into the region introduced new cultures and ways of life to Canaan due to the arrival of the Israelites, the Philistines, who came from the Aegean region, and the Sea Peoples from the western Mediterranean.

The second half of the Iron Age began as the Israelites established the United Monarchy under King Saul, with the dynasty continuing until the kingdom split into Israel and Judah. Several other kingdoms emerged during this time, including Assyria and Babylon, which established their own empires in the region. The end of the second half of the Iron Age was followed by the Neo-Babylonian era, which marked the Babylonian attack on the Israelites. But let's start at the beginning.

Iron Age I

As the Bronze Age neared its end, Canaan became a rapidly deteriorating region. Much of the region had been abandoned, with settlements moving to more developed areas. The remaining cities that still retained some people shrank significantly in size. At the time of the Israelites' arrival, the entire region likely did not number more than 100,000 people. Most of this remaining population was concentrated along coastal plains or communication routes. The area the Israelites would later occupy was hilly and removed from open routes; therefore, the area was sparsely populated at the time.

As Canaan deteriorated, so did its cultural and political systems. Any system that existed was abandoned near the end of the Bronze Age since the region became so sparsely populated. The movement of civilizations into the region, such as the Israelites, the Philistines, and the Phoenicians, redeveloped these systems. However, during the Bronze Age, the region struggled with a heavy Egyptian political influence due to Egyptian wars and incursions, which led to much unrest and conflict.

These new civilizations, including the Israelites, began to settle in Canaan, and the social makeup of the region changed. The number of villages in Canaan grew exponentially, going from twenty-five to over three hundred by the end of the first half of the Iron Age. While the density of these villages was greater in the north, where the Israelites are believed to have encamped, no archaeological evidence has been uncovered that could definitively point to Israelite residence in this area. While some historians are attempting to reach such conclusions based on the animal remains or pottery styles unearthed at these sites, it is hard to state with any certainty that Israelite tribes did settle in this region of Canaan.

However, attempts to determine ethnic identity have established some patterns that are consistently found in areas believed to have been occupied by the Israelites. Some common factors that have been identified are the lack of pig bones, pottery with more significant decorative designs than others found in the Canaan region, the practice of circumcision, and a period marked with prohibitive practices, the influence of religion, and the importance of family and genealogy.

Aspects of Israelite society uncovered through archaeological excavations suggest the tribes lived in village centers with small populations, with barely over three hundred to four hundred people belonging to each village. The tribes sustained themselves through farming and herding. Although the tribes lived off of limited resources, they were self-sustaining, and economic trade between them was prevalent. Accounts also suggest the village tribes were led by appointed chieftains who provided leadership and security to the unwalled villages.

Iron Age II

The Hebrew Bible indicates the formation of the United Monarchy as early as the 11th century BCE, which developed under the rule of Saul, David, and Solomon. When this united kingdom split, it gave the cities of Shechem and Samaria, which had been part of the settlements of ten of the twelve tribes in the north, to the Kingdom of Israel. The remaining two tribes, along with Jerusalem and the Jewish Temple in the Kingdom of Judah, were established to the south. While sufficient archaeological evidence has been discovered indicating the existence of the United Monarchy, historians are divided on its dating, although many agree that the separate states of Israel and Judah existed by the 9th century BCE at the latest.

During the first two centuries of the Iron Age II, a population and settlement expansion occurred in the region. The unified kingdom made Samaria its capital, existing in relative peace and experiencing economic prosperity. Sometime between the 11th and 10th centuries BCE, Israel transformed from a settlement of nomadic tribes to an independent state and was often engaged in territorial disputes with neighboring nations, such as the Egyptians.

Judah's emergence as an independent entity occurred later and initially consisted of only small unguarded settlements. During the reign of Hezekiah, in the 8th century BCE, Judah grew to become a great power; meanwhile, Israel was falling to foreign attacks. However, before this period, Israel was the more prosperous of the two, with improved infrastructure and great urban development. Judah's economy was less developed and much smaller. It did not achieve a more advanced or dominant status until the 7th century, possibly as an Assyrian vassal state.

Much of Judah's development can be attributed to the efforts of King Josiah in the mid-7th century. Religious reforms were introduced, with Josiah attempting to centralize worship in the Temple in Jerusalem, extinguishing other forms of worship within Judah. Josiah sought a truly monotheistic religion with the worship of Yahweh. While a new temple was constructed in Judah, sites of other religious worship were destroyed.

Some historians suggest this may have been, at least in part, a political move, with the Judeans seeking to establish harmony with the Babylonians by imitating their style of temple worship since Babylonia was the central power of the region at the time. These efforts proved futile, as Judah was invaded under Babylonian King Nebuchadnezzar II at the beginning of the 6th century BCE. This invasion led to the destruction of the First Temple (the Temple in Jerusalem) and the forced mass deportation of the Judeans in a period known as the Babylonian exile or the Babylonian captivity.

During this period of forced exile, the Judeans attempted to maintain their religious and cultural identity, despite being far away from home and living in slavery. Only after they were freed by Cyrus the Great during his conquest of Babylon were the Judeans able to return home. They immediately turned their attention toward the restoration of the destroyed temple and the construction of a new one.

Campaign of Shoshenq I

Archaeological evidence has shown the true extent of Egyptian Pharaoh Shoshenq I's invasion of the eastern Mediterranean region. Between the years 930 and 925 BCE, he invaded the Levant, capturing many cities and conquering settlements in the process. Rather than annex the Levant, Shoshenq I chose to enforce exile on its people, bringing them under Egyptian dominion. While the reasoning behind this move remains uncertain, historians suggest this might have been to derail the force of a unified state under Israelite rule, which Shoshenq I likely perceived as a threat.

Details of Shoshenq I's campaign against Israel vary, depending on whether you look at archaeological evidence or biblical accounts. For instance, the account of the campaign in the Bible refers to Jerusalem as the primary target. However, the recovered triumphal relief of Shoshenq I indicates the campaign was largely concentrated in the lands that were part of the Kingdom of Israel.

The Book of Kings narrates the arrival of Shoshenq I and recounts his success in taking the treasures from the palace and the Temple of Jerusalem for himself. The Kingdom of Israel might have been brought to Shoshenq I's attention during the reign of Solomon, at least based on biblical accounts.

This might have occurred when Solomon attempted to put Jeroboam, an administrator, to death on account of treason. However, Jeroboam fled to Egypt, where he was granted asylum in Shoshenq's court. Following the death of Solomon, Jeroboam returned to Israel, where he managed to force the assembly to reject Rehoboam, the son and successor to Solomon, instead instating himself as king.

Other accounts suggest a political bond existed between Egypt and Israel because of Solomon's marriage to the pharaoh's daughter, though it must be noted that no archaeological evidence has been discovered indicating such an alliance. However, harboring fugitives of Israel appears to have been an Egyptian policy that caused havoc in the region, as the Egyptian treaty with Israel existed only with David and Solomon. Egypt also supported the split of Israel from Judah, which was a political move since the split made Israel weaker compared to the might of Egypt.

The split of the monarchy provided Egypt with a lucrative opportunity to take control of the region. Some evidence suggests the destruction of Israel by the Egyptians might have been greatly exaggerated. However, it is true that after the kingship of Jeroboam, Israel became a vassal state to the Egyptians and lost much of its power.

The Assyrian Invasion

Shalmaneser III.
Osama Shukir Muhammed Amin FRCP(Glasg), CC BY-SA 4.0 <https://creativecommons.org/licenses/by-sa/4.0>, via Wikimedia Commons; https://commons.wikimedia.org/wiki/File:Shalmaneser_III,_detail,_North_Face,_East_End,_Throne_Dais_of_Shalmaneser_III_from_Nimrud,_Iraq.jpg

Assyrian power began to rise in the Near East in the 21st century BCE, although it would rise and fall several times as the centuries passed. By the mid-8th century BCE, the Neo-Assyrian Empire had conquered much of the Middle East. Because of its formidable kings, the nation was able to increase its power and establish itself as an empire through the expansion of its borders, going on to rule parts or all of Babylonia, Armenia, Media, Judah, Syria, Phoenicia, Sumeria, Elam, and Egypt. Assyrian warfare was the apex of efficiency and complexity, and the Assyrians were also known for their savagery in war. Their reputation brought fear into the hearts of their enemies.

The Battle of Qarqar

In 853 BCE, Shalmaneser III and his Assyrian army fought against an allied force of eleven kings led by the kings of Damascus and Israel at Qarqar. The other allies included Arabia, Ammon, Usnatu, Arwad, and Hamath.

Shalmaneser's account of the battle relates that he inflicted close to fourteen thousand casualties, resulting in a definitive victory for the Assyrians. However, such accounts are often unreliable, as rulers tend to exaggerate their victories and the results of battles. The Battle of Qarqar's only known account comes from the Kurkh Stela, the Assyrian stela narrating Shalmaneser's rule. Whether a victory was indeed achieved, the Assyrians did not conquer any more lands in the region until the years following 840 BCE.

The Destruction of Israel

At the time of Assyria's march against Israel, the empire was at the height of its power. Its reputation for brutality and savagery was well known. Meanwhile, Israelite society had strayed away from its religious principles and forgotten the monotheistic worship of Yahweh. As a result, the Israelites were repeatedly warned by the Prophet Isaiah of the doom that awaited them if they did not repent.

Around 738 BCE, the Assyrians received tribute from Syria and Samaria, the Israelite capital. Four years later, a rebellion in Damascus spurred an Assyrian invasion, which also led to the loss of some Israelite territories in the north. The revolt of Israelite King Hoshea against the Assyrians led to the siege of Samaria around 722 BCE by Shalmaneser V, which went on for three years. During this time, Shalmaneser died, and Sargon II took the throne in his place. The credit for the siege varies, as Sargon claimed to have conquered Samaria, yet historians believe Shalmaneser had managed to do so before his death and that Sargon took credit for it. However, it is possible that Sargon recaptured the city after a brief rebellion. Regardless, the siege of Samaria was successful, and following the fall of the city, Israel was destroyed. Its inhabitants were shipped off to Assyria in captivity and were resettled in various lands, resulting in the loss of the ten tribes of Israel.

The Babylonian Invasion

The fall of the Kingdom of Israel to the Neo-Assyrians had consequences for the neighboring Kingdom of Judah as well, as it became a vassal state to the Neo-Assyrian Empire. The Assyrians abandoned any campaigns against Judah in favor of accepting the tribute the Judeans offered. Campaigns against the Judeans by the Babylonians later led to Judah becoming a Neo-Babylonian vassal state. However, unrest in the region continued, leading to the Babylonian invasion in 586 BCE. While historical accounts fail to provide sufficient information, biblical accounts suggest Judah was besieged by the Babylonians between 589 and 586 BCE. The invasion resulted in the destruction of the First Temple and the exile of the people of Judah. It was also during this time that the Yahwism religion morphed into the monotheistic religion of Judaism.

As a Babylonian vassal, Judah suffered greatly in terms of population and economy. During this time, its defenses were greatly weakened, so regions like Negev, Shephelah, and Hebron were lost to invasions from neighboring countries. Jerusalem, which had been the capital of a prosperous Judah, shrunk considerably in size, and Mizpah in the northern part of the Judean Kingdom was appointed the capital of Yehud, the name for the Babylonian province of Judah. To shift the religious significance of Jerusalem and the power of Judah, a new temple was constructed at Bethel in the province of Benjamin by those who had been left behind, replacing the one destroyed in Jerusalem.

The Babylonian invasion of Judah sought to establish Babylonian dominance over the region and cripple its religious infrastructure. The most significant attempt in doing so was challenging the belief that Jerusalem was the promised land Yahweh had set aside for the Israelites, his chosen people. The fall of the region to foreign invaders introduced a religious crisis of sorts, forcing kings, scribes, and prophets to conceptualize their understanding of their faith.

However, the monotheism of their religion evolved, focusing more on concepts of individual responsibility and universalism. There was also a greater emphasis on individual purity and holiness. The exile of the Judeans also had the effect of fostering a greater sense of religious identity among its people, setting them apart from the Babylonians with whom they were forced to live. The Judeans continued to observe their religion, marking their separation from other groups by observing the Sabbath and continuing the practice of circumcision in secret.

Conflicting archaeological evidence suggests different accounts of the social structure of Neo-Babylonian Judah. Some historians suggest that much of Judah's population was allowed to remain in their homeland, with life continuing like it had before or even better since they were rewarded with the lands of those who had been deported to Babylonia. Many of those who were deported owned lands or held influence over the people. Other accounts suggest that Judah was almost completely depopulated following the Babylonian invasion, with nearly fourteen thousand to eighteen thousand people being exiled, leaving barely 10 percent of the original population behind.

Chapter 4: Biblical References to Ancient Israel

Israel's religious history as the holy land means it has great biblical significance. The land of Israel forms the foundation of the Bible and the Judean and Christian faiths, so it holds great importance for many. As such, it is essential to understand the way the Bible references and discusses this holy land, its people, and their way of living.

Many tales of ancient Israel can be found in biblical texts, particularly with regard to its kings. Their rule is narrated almost entirely within biblical references, as little to no outside sources exist that narrate information relating to the kings of the United Monarchy. Thus, these biblical references are an important historical testimonial to the state of the monarchy and the Golden Age of Israel.

The United Monarchy

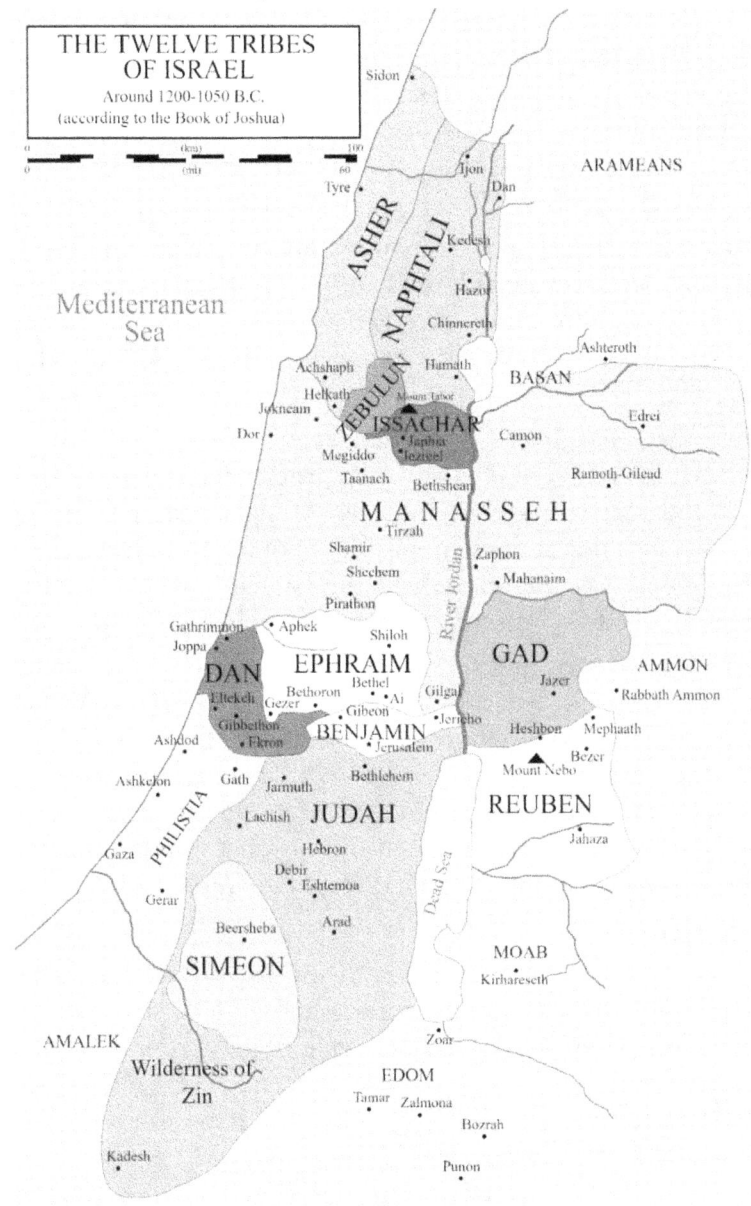

The twelve tribes of Israel.
12 tribus de Israel.svg: Translated by Kordas12 staemme israels heb.svg: by user:12שי staemme israels.png: by user;Janzderivative work Richardprins, CC BY-SA 3.0 <http://creativecommons.org/licenses/by-sa/3.0/>, via Wikimedia Commons; https://commons.wikimedia.org/wiki/File:12_Tribes_of_Israel_Map.svg

The story of Israel, as narrated by the Old Testament, starts with the covenant made at Mount Sinai following the freedom of the Israelite people from Egyptian slavery. Israelites were given the opportunity to accept God (Yahweh) and to live as his chosen people. If they accepted, he would lead them to the promised land. The Ten Commandments were then revealed to the people, along with the statutes offered by God that came to be known as the Book of the Covenant.

The teachings of the Ten Commandments are narrated in the Book of Exodus. The Ten Commandments forbid the worship of other gods, idols, or images and to take the Lord's name in vain. They also command the honor of one's parents and forbid theft, killing, adultery, greed, and lying.

Despite the Israelites' promises to adhere to the Ten Commandments, they were unable to stay true to their word. Instead of following God's commands, they were plagued by disbelief, disobedience, and the influence of the people around them. This disobedience is cited as the reason why the Israelites were not led to the promised land right away, entering Canaan around 1250 BCE.

For the next several hundred years, Israel existed as a civilization without a king, guided instead by prophets who had been sent by God to teach his people the right way to live. Eventually, the people of Israel requested a king from the Prophet Samuel. They wanted someone to pass judgment and rule the lands like their neighbors. This request is narrated in the Book of Samuel when the prophet asked God to heed the people's desires. Samuel was then directed to appoint Saul as king.

Reign of Saul

The kingship of Saul, which began in the late 11th century BCE, is largely considered the period when the scattered Israelite and Judean civilizations were united under a single rule. The accounts of his rule come largely from the Hebrew Bible, which speaks of his anointment by Samuel. Saul came from the Gibeah region, which was also the epicenter of his rule, and hailed from the tribe of Benjamin.

Accounts of Saul's rule and the length of his reign vary. Some biblical accounts suggest he only ruled for two years, but historians agree that his rule must have spanned between twenty to twenty-two years if he existed in the first place (there is no firm proof that the early Israelite kings existed, which is something that we will talk about later; the estimated years of Saul's rule come from other historical events that coincided with his reign). The New Testament suggests he ruled for forty years.

Three accounts of Saul's appointment as king are related in successive chapters of the Book of Samuel. One account suggests he was privately anointed by Samuel while he was out looking for his father's donkeys near Ramah. The second account narrates Samuel's attempt to find a king following the rising movement to establish a monarchy in Israel. Reportedly, Samuel gathered people by a tribe, settling on the Benjamin tribe, and then by a clan, choosing the Matri, from among whom Saul was selected. A third account speaks of Saul leading an army against the Ammonites, who had laid siege to Jabesh-Gilead in northwest Jordan. Returning victorious, the Israelites gathered in Gilgal and crowned Saul king.

Following this victory, Saul led many more military campaigns, which the Bible suggests all resulted in victories. This includes campaigns against Aram Rehob, the Edomites, the Moabites, the Ammonites, the Amalekites, the Philistines, and the Aram-Zobah. His victory against the Philistines in the second year of his rule was particularly remarkable, as he led a few thousand Israelite soldiers to victory against a massive Philistine force that was about forty thousand strong.

The Philistines were a group of non-Semitic people who had settled on the southern coast of Canaan in Philistia. Their mention in the Old Testament is largely concerned with their frequent wars with the Israelites. The causes of their frequent clashes are mostly attributed to the violent lifestyle and warring tendencies of the Philistines. Their expansionist policies and differences with the Israelites, particularly with their practice of religion and social structure as a non-unified state, might have also encouraged hostilities.

The beginning of Saul's demise as ruler came after his falling-out with Samuel, who had instructed Saul to lead an army against the Amalekites and completely destroy them. While Saul did so, killing their men, women, children, and poorest livestock, he spared the king and their best livestock. When Samuel learned Saul had disobeyed him, he told Saul that God rejected him as king. When Saul seized Samuel's garments and tore them in anger, Samuel prophesized the end of Saul's rule.

Samuel then sought out David, son of Jesse and servant to Saul, and anointed him king in front of his brothers. For the remainder of Saul's rule, Saul remained distrustful of David, even attempting to have him killed on several occasions.

Saul's end came with the Battle of Gilboa, where the Philistines had gathered to launch an attack against the Israelites. Before the battle, Saul visited a witch who conjured the spirit of Samuel, who had died five years previously. He informed Saul that God had forsaken him and that he would lose both the battle and his life the next day.

While accounts vary slightly, the most common narration suggests that Saul died by suicide during battle, falling on his own sword. The Philistines took hold of the bodies of Saul and his slain brothers from the battlefield and displayed their decapitated heads on the walls of Bethshan.

Eshbaal Takes Over

Eshbaal, or Ish-bosheth, as he is referred to in the Hebrew Bible, was the second monarch of the Kingdom of Israel, succeeding his father Saul around 1012 BCE. His two-year reign was mostly punctuated by battles and conflicts with David, who received much support. Following the death of Saul, Saul's army captain, Abner, instated Eshbaal as the new king. However, the tribe of Judah opposed this appointment, instating David as their king, which led to a war.

The war concluded in David's favor when Abner deserted Eshbaal. David's terms of peace included the return of his wife, Michal, daughter of Saul and sister of Eshbaal. Michal had been given away by Saul to another man after David was forced to flee.

Eshbaal's short-lived rule is also narrated in the Book of Samuel, which speaks of his assassination. He was killed by two of his army captains, Rechab and Baanah, who committed treason in the hopes of a reward from David. However, David refused to reward them, instead ordering their execution. He had their hands and feet cut off.

The Golden Age of Israel

The Golden Age of the Kingdom of Israel is believed to have started with the rule of David. During this time, the kingdom achieved great wealth, prosperity, and splendor. Israel's economic and religious prosperity, along with the development of effective trade relations and the wisdom of its rulers, made it a notable force in the region. Its Golden Age might have been too dependent on its rulers, though, as the end of Solomon's rule marked the decline of the period. However, Israel prospered while it lasted.

David Becomes King

David fighting Goliath.
Majumwo, CC BY-SA 4.0 <https://creativecommons.org/licenses/by-sa/4.0>, via Wikimedia Commons; https://commons.wikimedia.org/wiki/File:David_as_he_fights_Goliath.jpeg

After the death of Eshbaal, David was accepted as king of the Kingdom of Israel around 1010 BCE. According to the Bible, David would have already been a well-known figure. During the reign of Saul, David had been a favorite of the king as an accomplished harpist and the man who defeated the Philistine giant Goliath in battle. Goliath challenged the Israelites to send out a champion who would dare face him. Saul was afraid, but David volunteered, taking only a staff, a sling, and five stones with him.

It appeared to be an unfair confrontation since Goliath was many times the size of David. Goliath had armor and a javelin, while David had little to fight with other than stones. Yet David scored a victory when he slung a stone, hitting Goliath in the center of his forehead, causing him to fall to the ground. David then cut off his head, causing the Philistines to flee, with the Israelites chasing after them.

David even became close friends with Saul's son, Jonathan. However, once Samuel declared Saul was no longer in God's favor, Saul became increasingly paranoid about David stealing his throne and made multiple attempts to assassinate him.

David's most notable achievement after becoming king was his conquest of Jerusalem, which had been under the control of a Canaanite tribe called the Jebusites. He was also able to return the Ark of the Covenant to Israel, which had resided in Shiloh. The Ark was later placed in the First Temple by King Solomon. David, who already held much fame and support among the Israelites, became even more popular with his conquests over the Moabites, the Amalekites, the Philistines, the Ammonites, the Edomites, and the Aram-Zobah.

The First Book of Samuel and the Book of Chronicles narrate David's family life. While his armies laid siege to Rabbah in Ammon, David remained in Jerusalem, where he met Bathsheba, whom he impregnated. He later had her husband killed in the guise of battle. However, after acknowledging his sin to the Prophet Nathan, he was told that his child would not survive. David also faced revolts from his own sons. First, his favorite son, Absalom, rose up in vengeance against him, killing David's other son, Ammon, for raping his sister. Absalom's plans against his father might have been successful had he not been infiltrated by David's men. Absalom was caught in the Wood of Ephraim. Despite David's orders against a severe punishment, Absalom was killed for his treachery. David mourned him greatly.

On David's deathbed, David's eldest son, Adonijah, declared himself king. However, Bathsheba and the Prophet Nathan convinced David to appoint Solomon, Bathsheba's son, as king. Adonijah's revolt was quickly suppressed. Thus, Solomon became king following the death of David at the age of seventy. Solomon's rule might have been directly influenced by David, whose parting words to his son were to seek revenge on his behalf.

David plays a significant role in the biblical narrative and religious mythology. Jewish tradition represents David as the ideal king and as the ancestor to Jesus, which is mentioned in the Gospels of Matthew and Luke. Islamic tradition also shows David as both the king of Israel and a prophet of God. However, it must be remembered that the information in this chapter comes from the Old Testament; there is no firm historical evidence that David ever existed, although most scholars do agree that David and Solomon were real people. We will dive into the historicity of these rulers later in the chapter and provide some evidence for their possible existence.

Solomon Takes the Throne

A depiction of the Temple of Solomon at Jerusalem.
Wellcome Images, CC BY 4.0 <https://creativecommons.org/licenses/by/4.0>, via Wikimedia Commons; https://commons.wikimedia.org/wiki/File:The_temple_of_Solomon_at_Jerusalem._Coloured_engraving,_ca._Wellcome_L0047683.jpg

The Golden Age of Israel is said to have begun with the rule of David, but the kingdom experienced even more prosperity under Solomon. However, the end of his reign also marked the decline of the United Monarchy. Solomon is believed to have taken the throne in the year 970 BCE following his father's death. He ruled for around forty years. The First Book of Kings references Solomon's rule and his demise.

Biblical and religious references portray Solomon as a prophet and a wise ruler. His wisdom is portrayed as a gift from God, who appeared to Solomon in a dream and asked what gift he wanted, to which Solomon requested wisdom to rule his people. His wealth and power are also referenced, and the Islamic tradition portrays him as a prophet of God. Even non-religious traditions refer to Solomon as a magician, attributing many amulets recovered from the Hellenistic period to him.

Solomon's first act as king was to follow his father's instructions and purge the kingdom of usurpers and treacherous individuals, taking out those who had opposed David or plotted against him. To guard his kingship, Solomon appointed trusted friends to important administrative, civic, military, and even religious posts. According to the Bible, Solomon built the First Temple of Jerusalem, which his father had wanted to construct, to store the Ark of the Covenant. The temple was dedicated to the worship of Yahweh. Solomon also built a royal palace in Jerusalem and rebuilt many cities, which aided in Israel's trade efforts.

Under Solomon's rule, the Israelite military was strengthened, particularly with the addition of chariots and cavalry. Solomon also established many trading and military posts by founding new colonies. He followed in his father's footsteps by focusing on developing and strengthening Israel's trade relations, particularly with the Phoenicians. He also cultivated trade relationships with Tarshish and Ophir, which brought luxury products like silver, gold, sandalwood, ivory, pearls, apes, and peacocks to the kingdom. Israel's flourishing economy and Solomon's vast wealth can be attributed to these successful trade contracts.

Solomon's wisdom was highly regarded and sought after. One of the most famous examples is the judgment of Solomon. You might be familiar with the story. Two women came to Solomon, both laying claim to a child. Solomon suggested cutting the child in half and giving each woman a part. One of the women protested, choosing instead to give up her claim. Solomon gave her the child, citing that only the real mother would rather give up her child than see it die. Solomon also authored several books, including the Wisdom of Solomon, the Song of Solomon, and the Books of Proverbs and Ecclesiastes.

Solomon eventually angered God, causing the United Monarchy to split. He turned away from God and instead worshiped the false gods of his wives, even going as far as to build temples for their worship. Solomon died at the age of sixty from natural causes. Following the pattern of the hereditary monarchy that had been established in Israel, his son, Rehoboam, took the throne. The end of Solomon's rule also marked the beginning of the end of the Golden Age of Israel, as the kingdom moved from development and prosperity to conflict and unrest.

The Last Ruler of the United Monarchy: King Rehoboam

Even before Solomon's death, the kingdom had begun to disintegrate. The First Book of Kings narrates that some of the unrest might have been caused by Solomon's practices in his personal life, which did not align with the religious beliefs of the land, such as his marriage to many foreign wives and the worship of Ammonite and Moabite gods.

When Rehoboam became king, he immediately faced opposition from ten of the Israelite tribes. Rehoboam's mother was Ammonite, making her one of Solomon's foreign wives. Therefore, her son, in the eyes of the Israelites, was not fit to rule. Rehoboam's reign, which is described in the Books of Kings and the Second Chronicles, is believed to have started in 931 BCE and lasted about twenty years.

While the Israelites objected to Rehoboam's heritage, the final straw might have happened at his coronation, when the ten tribes gathered to ask for certain reforms to be passed. Instead of engaging in a civil discussion, Rehoboam imposed heavier taxation on the tribes. This, coupled with the heavier economic burden on the tribes due to Solomon's lavish lifestyle, was not well received. In addition, the Israelite and Judean regions had historically harbored animosity toward one another, which had only been quelled when David united the two with his military victories. When the ten tribes rebelled, they broke apart from the United Monarchy, establishing the Kingdom of Israel and leaving Rehoboam to be the ruler of the smaller Kingdom of Judah. The two regions remained at war with each other throughout Rehoboam's reign.

Rehoboam's fifth year of rule was marked by the invasion of King Shishak of Egypt. The fifteen fortified cities built by Rehoboam during his rule suggest he had been expecting an attack; however, whether some previous altercation had led him to believe an attack from Egypt was imminent or if he was simply preparing for the possibility of war is not clear. Shishak took all of the fortified cities, forcing Rehoboam to surrender. Rehoboam offered all the riches from the Temple as tribute. From that point forward, Judah became a vassal state to Egypt. While historical records are unclear, many historians believe this Shishak, as mentioned in the Book of Chronicles, refers to Shoshenq I. At the end of Rehoboam's reign, his son, Abijah, succeeded him.

Historicity

As mentioned, there isn't any firm evidence that the United Monarchy ever existed. Some scholars believe there is evidence that it existed, such as parts of David's palace; however, other scholars are skeptical, saying the discovery could not be that. Some archaeologists believe they have found stones and stelae with David's name on them, although other scholars believe the name might relate to someone else or is translated incorrectly.

That being said, most scholars believe that David and Solomon existed. However, they don't believe they lived as lavishly as depicted in the Bible. Although there isn't any solid proof that the Davidic kings walked the earth, it is hard to entirely discount the biblical writings, which is why archaeologists and scholars are still trying to prove their existence today.

Chapter 5: The Kingdom of Judah

The Kingdom of Judah, just like its counterpart, was descended from the Israelites who had received guidance and the blessing of God on Mount Sinai. Initially, Judah was part of the United Monarchy (at least according to biblical tradition), but the tribes later split, with two of the tribes forming the Kingdom of Judah in the south. Even if the United Monarchy existed, it likely was only superficially united.

During the kingdom's early years, it remained sparsely populated. It wasn't until much later, under foreign rule, that it began to grow and prosper. Judah plays an important role in the lives of the Jews, who are primarily descended from the people of this region.

Jeroboam's Revolt

Even before the end of the United Monarchy and the formation of the separate Kingdom of Judah, friction existed between the southern region and the northern region. One reason for the tensions was the topography. Judah (the southern region) was isolated from the other ten tribes in the north due to mountains and valleys. The seclusion of Judah from the rest of the kingdom, combined with its shared border with the Philistines, who often clashed against the United Monarchy, did not help foster friendly relations.

The true divide between the regions came with the revolt of the ten Israelite tribes. It began with the coronation ceremony of Rehoboam, the last of the kings under the United Monarchy. At the ceremony, the ten Israelite tribes, led by Jeroboam, approached the newly anointed king and asked him to grant a reduction in the heavy taxes Solomon had levied to fund his lavish lifestyle. In response, Rehoboam chose to increase the taxes, causing the ten tribes to rebel. They appointed Jeroboam as their king around 931 BCE.

While only the tribe of Judah remained loyal to Rehoboam initially, the tribe of Benjamin soon joined to form the Kingdom of Judah. Whatever tensions had existed between the north and south before the split intensified.

Jerusalem: The Judean Capital

Reconstructed model of ancient Jerusalem.
Водник at ru.wikipedia, CC BY-SA 2.5 <https://creativecommons.org/licenses/by-sa/2.5>, via Wikimedia Commons;
https://commons.wikimedia.org/wiki/File:Reconstruction_model_of_Ancient_Jerusalem_in_Museum_of_David_Castle.jpg

Jerusalem acted as the capital of Judah for around four hundred years. Before the split of the United Monarchy, it had acted as an important cultural and religious center, particularly after the construction of Solomon's Temple, which became the main center of worship. During Solomon's reign, several other important buildings were constructed in Jerusalem, such as Solomon's palace, indicating the sociopolitical significance and religious importance of the city.

After the split of the United Monarchy, Jerusalem was a politically unstable region. Throughout the Kingdom of Judah's existence, it was attacked and pillaged by the Egyptians, the Neo-Assyrians, the

Philistines, the Arabs, and the Ethiopians. The presence of the Temple allowed Jerusalem to maintain its position as a religious center and a place for frequent pilgrimages. As such, it had a significant social and religious role to play until the Babylonian invasion, when the city was completely laid to waste.

Following the freedom of the Judeans from the Babylonian captivity by Cyrus the Great, the Jews were allowed to return home, and the Achaemenid king offered monetary help in rebuilding the city. The construction of the Second Temple was completed during the reign of the third emperor of the Achaemenid Empire, Darius the Great, and the walls of the city were rebuilt with the aid of Artaxerxes I, his successor. Jerusalem was restored, and its people lived in relative peace until the Greeks defeated the Achaemenids and took over the Persian Empire.

Life in Judah

After the split of the United Monarchy, Israel and Judah remained at odds with each other, and they were engaged in a civil war throughout Rehoboam's reign. Since Rehoboam had been initially appointed king of the United Monarchy, not just of Judah, he made efforts to bring Israel under his control and built many fortified cities in preparation for war. Rehoboam's son also sought to bring Israel under Judean rule.

While this civil war was going on, in the fifth year of Rehoboam's rule, Judah was invaded by Pharaoh Shoshenq I of Egypt, who brought down the fortified cities of Judah with ease. In response, Rehoboam chose to surrender rather than fight, giving Shoshenq the treasures from the Temple of Jerusalem as tribute. Having conquered the region, Shoshenq allowed the Judeans to continue living as they had, except it was now a vassal state to Egypt. The vassal state continued its efforts to bring Israel under its realm.

Battle of Mount Zemaraim

Rehoboam was prepared to go to war against the newly established Kingdom of Israel when it first split, but he was counseled to refrain from going to war against his brethren. However, his son and successor, Abijah, led a historic battle against the Israelites at Mount Zemaraim. This battle is narrated in the Book of Chronicles and is believed to have taken place around 913 BCE.

In the Bible, Abijah is said to have led an army of 400,000 men against Israel's Jeroboam, who led around 800,000 men to settle disputes between the two kingdoms, most importantly the border issue. Before the battle, the Bible narrates that Abijah attempted to encourage the Israelites to lay down their arms and return to living under a unified rule. Jeroboam ignored the invitation and instead attempted an ambush maneuver against the Judeans, with a part of his army coming up behind them. However, Abijah was able to counter this move, turning the tables on the Israelites.

The Judeans earned a decisive victory in this battle, killing some 500,000 Israelites and giving chase to the remaining men who attempted to flee the battlefield. The Judeans were able to take the Israelite cities of Ephron, Bethel, and Jeshanah. While the battle was a conclusive win for Judah, it was not sufficient enough to reunite the two kingdoms and only served to deepen the hostilities between each other, with continuous border wars between the regions occurring until the Assyrians took over the Kingdom of Israel.

Battle of Zephath

After the confrontation at Mount Zemaraim, the two kingdoms did not engage in any major battles for a while. Abijah's successor, Asa, managed to maintain relative peace during the first few years of his rule until the Ethiopians, who were backed by the Egyptians, who sought to take direct control of the region, attacked the Judeans. The Second Book of Chronicles describes the Battle of Zephath, which took place in the Valley of Zephath in modern-day Israel.

The Ethiopians, led by Zerah, were about a million men in strength, according to the Bible, which states divine intervention as the reason behind the Judeans' victory in the battle. The Judeans pursued the Ethiopians as far as Gerar, where they had to stop out of exhaustion. Asa collected a significant number of treasures as a result of his victory and was able to establish peace with the Egyptians until the mid-7th century BCE.

Shaky Alliance with Israel

King Asa was once again challenged by the Israelites, led by Basha, who forced Asa to pay a high tribute. In return, Asa bribed the Damascene king to break his treaty with the Israelites and invade the region. This attack forced the Israelites away from the Judean border. Asa's successor, Jehoshaphat, changed the Judean policy toward the Israelites, as he instead attempted to forge an alliance with them.

This alliance was initially made through marriage. As the Second Book of Chronicles states, Jehoshaphat married his son to the daughter of King Ahab of Israel. In the Battle of Ramoth-Gilead, Ahab sought to get land back from Syria, known as Aram-Damascus at the time, and he was helped by Jehoshaphat. However, the battle was lost. Syria held control of Ramoth-Gilead, and Ahab was seriously wounded in the battle and bled to death.

Jehoshaphat attempted to create an alliance with Ahab's successor, Ahaziah, to maintain trade relations and maritime commerce. Jehoshaphat later aided Jehoram of Israel against the Moabites, who had been under Israelite rule and had risen up in revolt. The rebellion was quickly suppressed but resulted in Jehoshaphat's hasty retreat from the uprising when the Moabite king offered his own son up for sacrifice.

Jehoram succeeded Jehoshaphat, and the Judean rule began to falter.[1] Though Jehoram was able to form an alliance with the Israelites by marrying Ahab's daughter, there was trouble at home. Edom, a land to the south, rebelled against Judean rule, and Jehoram was forced to declare it an independent state. Further raids and attacks by the Arabs, the Ethiopians, and the Philistines took everything from the king's wealth to his family, leaving Judah in a weakened position.

Israel Falls

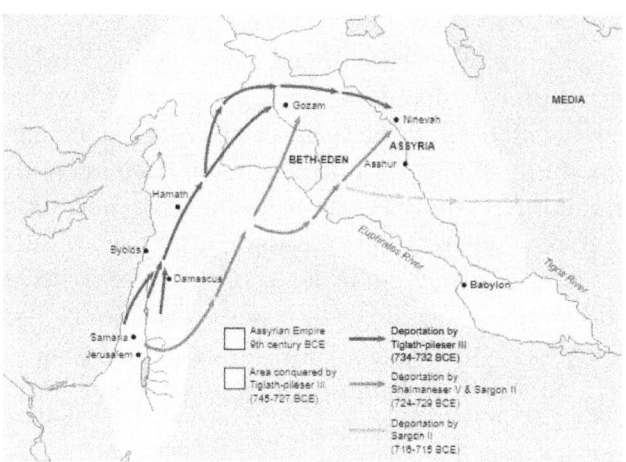

Deportations by Assyria.
Joelholdsworth, CC BY-SA 3.0 <http://creativecommons.org/licenses/by-sa/3.0/>, via Wikimedia Commons; https://commons.wikimedia.org/wiki/File:Deportation_of_Jews_by_Assyrians.svg

---

[1] Even biblical scholars are confused about who Jehoram (or Joram) was. The Bible mentions a Jehoram of Israel and a Jehoram of Judah. They reigned at the same time. So, does this mean they were the same person? Did the events get copied down incorrectly? Or was it just a coincidence that two Jehorams ruled at the same time?

Around the mid-8th century BCE, Israel was struggling against Neo-Assyrian incursions. The Book of Chronicles and the Second Book of Kings describe the relocation policy the Neo-Assyrian Empire initiated against the Israelites, which resulted in the demise of the Kingdom of Israel.

Israel was conquered by Shalmaneser V, and a period of forced removal of Israelites from their home to Assyria began. The deportations began in 732 BCE, and the Assyrians slowly conquered various Israelite cities. In 722 BCE, the city of Samaria, the capital of the Kingdom of Israel, fell to Sargon II after a three-year siege that was started by Shalmaneser V.

After hearing the news of Israel's fall, Hezekiah, King of Judah, opened up his land to the Israelites who had been left behind by the Assyrians. He wanted to hold Passover in Jerusalem. While some mocked this invitation, many Israelites who remained showed up, including those from Ephraim, Zebulun, Manasseh, and Issachar. Many historians are now of the belief that instead of the Assyrians taking all of the Israelites into their land, some of these regions were annexed by the Judeans, and the Israelites were absorbed into the Judean population following the Assyrian exile.

Unlike the Judeans, who were forced into exile by Babylonia but were able to return home generations later, the Israelites never returned. Thus, they are called the Ten Lost Tribes of Israel, and historical accounts suggest the Israelite population might have been absorbed into the Assyrian and Judean populations or among neighboring regions since history makes no mention or shows any traces of any of the ten Israelite tribes after the Assyrian exile. While the Assyrians also attacked Judah and laid siege to Jerusalem, they never took over or attempted to destroy the kingdom. Instead, the Assyrians allowed Judah to operate as a vassal state, although it had to pay much tribute to maintain its freedom.

Judah as an Assyrian Vassal

The Second Book of Kings narrates the arrival of the Assyrians to the Levant under Sennacherib, who warned the Judeans they could not withstand an Assyrian attack by just relying on their god. In 715 BCE, Hezekiah forged alliances with Egypt and Ashkelon, a Philistine region, to gather a force that would take a stand against the Assyrians by refusing to pay tribute. Sennacherib laid siege to Judah, and Hezekiah was forced to pay a high tribute, including all of the gold from the treasury of the Temple. He even stripped the gold from the doors of the Temple. Fourteen years later, Sennacherib again laid siege to Jerusalem, but he never took the city.

Throughout the rule of Manasseh, between the early 7th century BCE to about the mid-7th century BCE, Judah remained a vassal state of the Assyrians. The tribute imposed on the Judeans included providing aid for construction projects and assisting in campaigns. In 640 BCE, Manasseh's successor, Josiah, found some leeway in self-government since the Assyrian Empire had been struggling, the Egyptians were attempting to reestablish their autonomy following Assyrian rule, and the Neo-Babylonians had not yet risen.

However, in 609 BCE, Egyptian Pharaoh Necho II aided the Assyrians in leading an army into the Levant, entering through Syria. He was blocked in the Jezreel Valley by the Judeans, who were trying to aid the Babylonians by blocking Necho's path. However, in the ensuing battle, Josiah was slain, and the Egyptian-Assyrian alliance went on to lay siege to Harran, though they failed to keep their hold on the city. Necho II retreated to Syria.

Once Necho returned to Egypt, he replaced Josiah's successor, Jehoahaz, with Jehoahaz's older brother, Jehoiakim. Jehoahaz was taken as a prisoner to Egypt. As punishment, a heavy tribute was placed on Judah, which Jehoiakim was forced to pay until the Babylonians defeated the Egyptians. In a strategic move, Jehoiakim changed his allegiance and began paying tribute to Nebuchadnezzar II of Babylonia in 605 BCE.

In 601 BCE, Nebuchadnezzar led a failed campaign to take over Egypt, which also resulted in high losses for him. After seeing this failure, many of the Babylonian vassal states rebelled, including Judah. Jehoiakim refused to pay further tribute to the Babylonians. In response, Nebuchadnezzar laid siege to Jerusalem, attempting to quash the rebellion.

Siege of Jerusalem

The Flight of the Prisoners *by James Tissot.*
https://commons.wikimedia.org/wiki/File:Tissot_The_Flight_of_the_Prisoners.jpg

The Judean revolt against Babylonia lasted from around 601 BCE to about 586 BCE when Judah was taken over by the Babylonians. In 601 BCE, Jehoiakim died and was succeeded by his son, Jeconiah. In the first siege of Jerusalem in 597 BCE, the city surrendered. Jerusalem was looted by the Babylonians, and many prominent members, including the king himself, were deported. Jeconiah's uncle, Zedekiah, was installed as a vassal king.

The Book of Kings suggests this first siege lasted three months before the city surrendered and lost many of its riches and people, most notably the royalty and many skilled craftsmen. For about ten years, Judah remained a struggling state and a vassal to the Babylonians. Around 589 BCE, against the advice of the Prophet Jeremiah, Zedekiah forged an alliance with the Egyptians and revolted against the Babylonians.

In that same year, Nebuchadnezzar returned to Jerusalem and laid siege to the city again. The siege might have lasted somewhere between eighteen to thirty months and resulted in many Judeans escaping to neighboring regions to seek refuge. Those who remained behind suffered terribly, as they were deprived of many essentials. When Nebuchadnezzar finally broke through the defenses of the city, he captured Zedekiah, who had attempted to escape with his people. After being forced to watch his sons be killed, Zedekiah was blinded and taken captive to Babylonia, where he later died.

The Babylonians then initiated the complete destruction of Jerusalem. The Temple and the city were utterly destroyed, and most of the Judean population was taken as captives to Babylon. To complete the city's destruction, it was set ablaze, as were the surrounding towns and regions. A few Judeans were left behind to tend to the lands of the province of Yehud, and Gedaliah was appointed governor of the region.

Gedaliah was a native Judean, and the news of his appointment encouraged many Judeans who had sought refuge in neighboring lands to return to Judah. However, the assassination of Gedaliah at the hands of Ishmael of the royal house of Judah did not bring about any good feelings, and many of those who had returned made a hasty escape. Many sought refuge in Egypt, settling near the Nile. Judah remained a Babylonian province until the fall of Babylonia at the hands of Cyrus the Great.

The Yehud Province

Under the Babylonians, the town of Mizpah was appointed the capital of Yehud. Jerusalem, which had been completely destroyed, had no population to speak of during this time.

The ruling elite and the people in power were immediately removed and exiled to Babylon, which was the Babylonians' standard move when taking over regions. They wanted to ensure the conquered people would not incite a rebellion. Some people were left behind to tend to the lands, and the administrative capital was shifted to remove any power, symbolic or actual, from the previous center. And this move was effective, as the Jews were unable to rise against the Babylonians.

Nothing remarkable happened in Yehud throughout the 6th century BCE. However, after the fall of the Babylonians and the return of the exiled, Yehud Medinata emerged as an active sociopolitical sphere. It operated in relative autonomy, as it was allowed to function by its own laws, although it was obligated to pay tribute to the Persians.

Chapter 6: The Persian Period

Following the fall of Babylon to the Achaemenid Empire and the liberation of the Judeans in 539 BCE, Yehud Medinata was established during the Persian period as an autonomous Jewish province. It became an important administrative center within the Persian Empire and played a significant role in the rehabilitation of the Israelites following their forced exile.

Following the death of Cyrus the Great, a period of unrest occurred under his successor and son, Cambyses. Stability returned to the region with the rule of Darius I, who introduced tighter administrative controls in all Persian-held domains, including Yehud Medinata. Such controls were tightened further when the Persians temporarily lost Egypt. During this period, distinct religious, cultural, and administrative changes took place in Judean life, which were influenced by Persian rule.

The Formation of Yehud Medinata

Yehud Medinata highlighted in pink.
https://commons.wikimedia.org/wiki/File:Palestine_under_the_Persians_Smith_1915.jpg

Yehud Medinata came into existence following Cyrus the Great's conquest of Babylon when he allowed the Israelites to return home. One of his first acts following the conquest was to commission the rebuilding of their homeland, including the destroyed Temple, which is believed to have been restored sometime around 515 BCE.

Yehud Medinata was established as a Jewish province that operated under the watchful eye of the Achaemenid Empire. Its population numbered around thirty thousand people, and it remained a relatively small region. It was not until the mid-5th century BCE that Jerusalem was restored to its former political influence. Until then, Yehud Medinata remained a theocratic state ruled by high priests and Persian-appointed Jewish governors whose job was to maintain peace in the region and ensure the collection of tribute.

The Achaemenid Empire instated a policy of religious and cultural tolerance and did not impose its own religious practices on conquered lands. In the mid-5th century BCE, during Artaxerxes I's reign, the priests Ezra and Nehemiah were sent to Jerusalem to act in a priestly capacity and as governor to oversee the restoration of Jerusalem. Yehud Medinata had been experiencing civil unrest since the return of the exiled Jews, and Nehemiah expressed sorrow over how long it was taking to restore the walls of Jerusalem.

The unrest was caused by tensions between those who had returned and those who had stayed during the Babylonian captivity. The tensions might have been caused, at least in part, by the attitude of exclusivism that the returnees adopted during their exile in Babylon, as they had set themselves apart from their captors to maintain their sense of identity and culture. Back home, this exclusivity clashed with the people who lived there, leading to frequent conflicts. The unrest also might have been caused by the redistribution of property that took place following the exile, an issue that lay in dispute now that the returnees attempted to lay claim to their former lands. The arrival of Ezra and Nehemiah was intended to resolve these conflicts, helping the returnees to reintegrate into Jewish society and return to their religious practice.

During the Babylonian exile in the early 6th century BCE, Judah experienced a steep decline. The country's elite, the royal family, and the priesthood were all forced out of Judah. As a result, the economy suffered greatly, and any progress Judah had made following the devastation of Israel was lost. Gedaliah, a native of Judah, was instated as a puppet king in what was known as Yehud. The administrative center was moved from Jerusalem to Mizpah due to the destruction of Jerusalem and to perhaps break the consolidated power that had existed there. The province of Yehud also included the towns of Bethel, Mizpah, Jericho, Beth-Zur, and En-Gedi.

The arrival of the Babylonians in Judah spurred a refugee movement in the region, with many Judeans escaping and seeking refuge in surrounding areas. When the news of Gedaliah's appointment reached them, many returned to Yehud. However, unrest soon followed when Gedaliah was assassinated. The Babylonian garrison attacked, and many of Yehud's inhabitants sought refuge in Egypt.

It is difficult to establish the exact number of people who stayed behind in Yehud, those who had been forcibly deported to Babylon, and those who escaped to Egypt and other nearby regions. In the Book of Jeremiah, it is stated that around 4,600 people were forced into exile in Babylonia. The earlier deportation of between eight thousand to ten thousand people by Nebuchadnezzar at the beginning of the 6th century adds to these figures, citing the complete destruction and alteration of the social atmosphere of Judah.

During the Persian era, between the years of 538 and 400 BCE, the unified religion that had begun to develop during the Babylonian captivity began to be practiced in Yehud Medinata. This largely happened because the Jews were given religious, social, and political independence by the Persians. This era also marked the beginning of the biblical canon. The Persian period had a profound impact on Judean life, religion, culture, and even language, and Persian policies changed the way the Judeans structured their life socially, politically, and economically. Hebrew, which had been the language of administration and the language of everyday use, was slowly replaced by Aramaic, the administrative language of the Persians, although Hebrew continued to be used in religious and social contexts.

The Organization of Yehud Medinata

Yehud Medinata developed largely under Persian influence; therefore, many Achaemenid policies determined the administrative, religious, and social organization of the region. For example, Darius I's reforms within the empire greatly influenced the writing, revisions, and organization of the Torah. Yehud Medinata consisted of the descendants from the Kingdom of Judah and the returnees liberated from the

Babylonian exile. The region also included an extensive Mesopotamian population, who joined the Jews from their much earlier exile to Samaria.

Administration in Yehud Medinata

Yehud coinage.
https://commons.wikimedia.org/wiki/File:YHD_coins.jpg

Compared to the former Kingdom of Judah, Yehud Medinata was significantly smaller, both in terms of population and geography. It stretched from Bethel in the east to the Jordan River and the Dead Sea in the south and toward the Judean highlands and coastal plains in the west. After Jerusalem was destroyed, it could no longer function as an administrative center, so the center shifted to Mizpah, which was located in the land of Benjamin.

Benjamin had been part of the Kingdom of Israel before its destruction and served better as an administrative region compared to Jerusalem because it was more densely populated. It became an important center, considering it held the new administrative city of Mizpah, as well as the religious center of Bethel. Mizpah retained this position of importance for over a century until 445 BCE when administrative control shifted back to Jerusalem.

It is unclear what administrative role Jerusalem played while Mizpah served as the main administrative city, but Jerusalem's destruction and severely reduced population likely meant it did not serve much of a governance purpose since it lacked any administrators or priestly bodies. However, with its reestablishment, it once again became the administrative center. Cyrus the Great sent a substantial sum of money out of his own revenue to fund the reconstruction of Jerusalem. The Jews were also allowed independent governance, and the tributes stolen out of Jerusalem by the Babylonians were returned to them. In return, the Jews had to pay tribute to the Persians. Jerusalem's walls were rebuilt, and the Second Temple was constructed, measuring about ninety feet high. From the late 5th century until the early 3rd century BCE, Jerusalem even held a local mint, striking silver coins.

Even with the rebuilding of the city, Jerusalem did not grow to a great size. It held anywhere between 500 to 1,500 citizens, a shadow of the population it had boasted before the invasion. However, Jerusalem, despite its size, was the only truly urban city in Yehud Medinata, as much of the rest of the region continued to live in small, unwalled villages. The entire region of Yehud Medinata never grew beyond thirty thousand in population. And while biblical accounts narrate mass migrations of Jews from Babylonia, there is little archaeological evidence to support this.

Governance of Yehud Medinata

Under Persian rule, the governors of Yehud Medinata were appointed from among the Jews, keeping in line with the Persian tradition of preserving the cultures of conquered lands. Cyrus the Great appointed Sheshbazzar as governor of Yehud in 538 BCE. Sheshbazzar was descended from the line of David. This line of governorship continued with his successor and nephew, Zerubbabel, although it is possible that Sheshbazzar and Zerubbabel were the same person. It is believed the Davidic line continued to serve as a governor until 500 BCE. The Persians implemented similar practices in other parts of the empire, such as Phoenicia, and while it might not have represented a restoration of the Davidic line, it did serve to maintain some peace in a region that abhorred foreign rule.

Yehud Medinata was also maintained by the high priest and prophets, emulating Judean practice before the Babylonian invasion. This succession is recorded in the Hebrew Bible in the Chronicles of Ezra and Nehemiah. However, the line of the Davidic succession, as well as the prophethood, ended by 500 BCE, leaving only the high priest in charge of governance. This led to Yehud Medinata being established as a theocracy ruled by a succession of high priests.

The governor of Yehud had the dual role of implementing both Israelite and Persian policies without doing injustice to either. Jewish customs noticeably included their religious practices, on which many political matters, such as the appointment and duties of the high priest, were based. Persian policies were largely focused on the collection of tribute from Jewish subjects. Thus, the people of Yehud Medinata were largely left to manage themselves. While a governor under the Persian Empire was typically assisted by a team of officials and scribes, no such assembly has been found to have existed in Yehud Medinata, perhaps marking another way in which the Jews were allowed to live independently under Persian rule. What can be said for certain is that most, if not all, of the governors of Yehud Medinata were Jewish. Artaxerxes I also removed the tribute obligation from those working in the Temple, a move that earned him great respect among the Jews.

Evolution of Religion

During the 10th and 7th centuries BCE, the Judean religion had not yet evolved into a monotheistic belief system and, therefore, largely operated as a henotheistic religion. While it revolved around the worship of Yahweh, it did not preclude the worship of other deities. This remained a point of contention within the Kingdoms of Israel and Judah since henotheistic worship went against the Ten Commandments and supposedly led to the doom of the Israelites, who fell to the Assyrians.

Monotheism had begun to emerge as a form of rebellion against Assyrian rule before the religion more fully formed into monotheism during the Babylonian exile. The Assyrians proclaimed their king to be the "Lord of the Four Quarters," with the four quarters referring to the four corners of the world, a title that was later taken by Cyrus the Great. This title seemed to challenge the concept of Yahweh for the Jews, who embraced the worship of one god as a rebellion. Following the Babylonian exile, Yahweh emerged more distinctly as the Judean god, and the other minor gods who had been previously worshiped as the sons of Yahweh were relegated to positions of angels or demons. This religious evolution began during the Babylonian period, but it continued to develop during the Persian and Hellenistic periods.

The Persian Empire was home to a mixture of religions, customs, cultures, and traditions, owing to the different lands, regions, and even empires that were conquered by the Achaemenids. The Achaemenids practiced Zoroastrianism, and undeniable influences can be seen in the evolution of Judaism and the religious beliefs and practices of Zoroastrianism.

The Babylonian exile and the later reintegration of the Jews in Yehud Medinata played a vital role in the development of the Jewish worldview, which was especially influenced by the reconstruction of Jerusalem and the Davidic line of governors that followed in the first few years of Persian rule. During their exile, a central tenet formed within Jewish life: the idea of exclusivity, which meant the Jews used their culture and religious practices to set themselves apart from the Babylonians.

When the Jews returned to their homeland (Yehud Medinata), they spread the belief that they were set apart from others. Even though both Ezra and Nehemiah are recorded to have expressed disdain at the emerging practice of Yahweh-worshipers marrying non-believers, they still maintained cordial relations with their neighbors. The monotheistic religion was open to all twelve tribes and any foreigners who wished to convert, but the title of Jew was reserved for the tribes of Judah and Benjamin and the holy tribe of Levi. While the religion was open to anyone, it did not grant everyone the same position within the religious hierarchy.

While much evidence suggests that the Yehudi religion evolved into a largely monotheistic form of worship during the period of Persian rule, some accounts do indicate that at least some Jews remained polytheistic. This practice might have emerged from a number of sociopolitical factors, including the exile and flight of many Jewish people to escape the Assyrians and, later, the Babylonians. Some Elephantine papyri indicate that a small community of Jews, who did not return from Elephantine to Yehud following the liberation of the Jews, believed in and worshiped Yahweh while also offering praise to the Egyptian goddess Anat. They even built a temple to worship her better. Following the end of Persian rule in Egypt, the Jewish temple in Elephantine was abandoned.

There is much evidence to suggest that the Torah underwent many alterations in terms of writing and its chronology during the Persian period. Some scholars believe this was the period when the final form of the Torah was determined, although others are of the view that its composition continued until the Hellenistic period. The changes that were implemented in the Torah during this time include the revision of history, spanning from ancient Israel all the way to the Kingdom of Judah. Older prophetic books, which had formed part of the Torah up until that time, were removed.

Language in Yehud Medinata

The Torah underwent a significant transformation from earlier writings after the liberation of Jews from Babylonian rule. Older works were revised, as well as accompanying interpretations. There were also passages and books that were not part of the earlier version. The consistent references to the Hebrew Bible in this version of the Torah suggest the Jews began to develop a greater sense of their scripture and holy writing and produced the work as a religious authority in the development of a monotheistic belief system.

The development and evolution of the written Jewish religion occurred alongside the transition of the written and administrative language. This influence was expected since the Persians conducted their administrative and diplomatic business in Aramaic as a way of unifying the various regions under a single banner. Having brought Aramaic into Yehud Medinata, it became vital to translate the Torah, though the book itself remained in Hebrew at this time, into Aramaic to make them accessible to Jews and other people, although certain sections, such as the Books of Daniel and Ezra, were originally written in Aramaic.

The language shift occurred to such a drastic degree that very few, if any, written materials in Hebrew survived from the Persian period. Most epigraphic materials that have been recovered were recorded in the Aramaic language, suggesting the wider prevalence of the language in Yehud Medinata. Aramaic continued to be used in the region long after the end of the Persian period, although Hebrew would be revived much later on.

The Persian Empire played a significant, if at times indirect, role in the development of culture, religion, and language. Persian political activities in other parts of the empire also influenced the Jews in important ways. Their religious practice was influenced by many factors and took on features of Persian worship, evolving into the form of Judaism known today.

The Persians' use of Aramaic in an administrative capacity necessitated the use of Aramaic within Yehud Medinata, changing the language of the Jewish people for centuries to come. As time passed, tension grew between the Persians and the Jews. These tensions were primarily caused by the plot concocted by Haman, a governor of the Achaemenid King Xerxes I, to murder the Jews of the Persian Empire. When Alexander the Great defeated the Achaemenids and took the Persian Empire for himself, these tensions ended, although new issues would soon arise.

Chapter 7: The Hellenistic Period (330–50 BCE)

The Achaemenid Empire lasted a little over two centuries, and in that time, it acquired and influenced many regions in the ancient Near East. The defeat of Babylonia toward the beginning of the empire allowed Cyrus the Great to liberate the Judeans held there in forced exile. He offered them the opportunity to return home, albeit under the influence of the Persian Empire. During this time, the Persian language, religion, and culture had a profound impact on Judean life.

The end of the Persian Empire came at the hands of Alexander the Great of Macedon, who faced the last Achaemenid king, Darius III, three times before gaining a sure victory over him. Alexander's rule over the Persian Empire also brought Yehud Medinata under his reign in 334 BCE. With Greek influence entering the region, the Hellenistic period began, resulting in the further evolution of Jewish thought and practice.

The Coming of the Hellenistic Period

The Hellenistic era in what had been the province of Yehud Medinata was comprised of four distinct phases. It began with the conquest of the Persian Empire and, by extension, present-day Palestine by Alexander the Great. Following his death, the Ptolemies took over at the beginning of the 3rd century BCE as an extension of the Ptolemaic rule in Egypt. At the end of the 3rd century BCE, the Seleucid rule from Mesopotamia extended to the region, lasting until the end of the 2nd century BCE. From then until the mid-1st century BCE, the Hasmoneans reigned in Judah, which came to be known as Judea in the Hellenistic period.

During the Hellenistic period, Judea was the central land between the Seleucid Empire in the west and the Ptolemaic Empire in the east. As a result, it was often caught up in the conflicts of neighboring empires, leading to a variety of rulers moving in and out of the region. However, in keeping with Persian tradition, Alexander the Great did not impose foreign rule over the Jews. Instead, Judea was ruled by the hereditary offices of the high priests, which was in line with the theocracy established in the region; however, Judea also acted as a Hellenistic vassal during this time.

Understandably, the arrival of a new people group brought new ideas and influences into Jewish lives, impacting their religion and customs. Hellenistic influences first emerged in Alexandria, Egypt, impacting the Egyptian Jews before later spreading to Judea. Most significantly, this cultural mix led to the translation of the Hebrew and Aramaic holy scripts into Greek, making it accessible to the newcomers and to the Alexandrian Jews, who could read neither Hebrew nor Aramaic.

During the Ptolemaic rule in Judea, which lasted between 301 and 198 BCE, there was relative peace in the region. A Jewish elite class emerged based on the people's involvement with the Ptolemaic Empire. They worked in administration and the military. This elite class lived under Hellenistic influence, so many Jewish practices became mixed with Hellenistic traditions. This period continued until the wars of Antiochus III, ruler of the Seleucid Empire, whose efforts led to Jerusalem falling under his rule in 198 BCE. Hellenization began during his reign, though it was mild and less enforced than compared to the rule of his successor.

Antiochus IV, his successor, did not uphold the values of religious freedom like Alexander the Great and the Ptolemies had. He looted the Temple in response to disturbances in Jerusalem, which occurred during his campaign in Egypt, causing him to divert his attention instead to the Jews. His response was to ban Jewish rites and traditions, effectively preventing the open practice of Jewish religious worship. Jewish resistance to Seleucid Hellenization led to further unrest and clashes between the Jews and the Seleucids, culminating in the Maccabean Revolt between the years 174 and 135 BCE. This led to the end of Seleucid rule over Judea, a victory marked by the celebration of

Hannukah today.

This rebellion within Judean lands, other than ending foreign rule over the Jews, also led to the formation of an independent Jewish kingdom, which was headed by the Hasmonaean dynasty. This dynasty emerged in 140 BCE and lasted as long as 37 BCE. Toward the dynasty's end, it was overrun by civil wars, which were perhaps influenced by the civil wars occurring in Rome at the same time. Although the Hasmonaean Kingdom emerged out of a rebellion against the Hellenization of Judea, the dynasty became increasingly Hellenistic. The Hasmonaean dynasty was ended by Herod, leading to the start of the Herodian dynasty, with the region becoming a vassal to Rome.

Alexander the Great's Influence on Judea

Alexander the Great.
British Museum, CC BY-SA 3.0 <https://creativecommons.org/licenses/by-sa/3.0>, via Wikimedia Commons; https://commons.wikimedia.org/wiki/File:Alexander_the_Great-British_Museum.jpg

Alexander the Great's invasion of the Persian Empire in 334 BCE and its subsequent conquest in 331 BCE had profound impacts on the cultural, ethnic, linguistic, and religious makeup of the region. It introduced Greek traditions into Persian life and the various regions that had been absorbed into the Persian Empire. While no evidence indicates that Alexander's expedition took him through Yehud

Medinata, his arrival still had a great influence on Jewish life and religion.

Around 332 BCE, Alexander the Great marched to Egypt, where he established Alexandria and visited the Oracle of Ammon. He was greeted by the local priest as a god, showing the acceptance of his rule by the Egyptians. Although Alexander marched through Palestine to get to Egypt, the evidence does not indicate he ever took the mountainous route that ran through Yehud Medinata to get there. Thus, there is no evidence that Alexander ever met with the Jews or had any direct interaction with them in Yehud Medinata.

Despite this, Alexander had a great impact on Jewish life. Most noticeably, he chose to leave Yehud Medinata as it was rather than imposing a new ruler on its people, which would most likely have resulted in rebellion and unrest in a region with a history of forced exile, slavery, and detestation for foreign rule. Alexander allowed the Jews to carry on as they were, simply replacing Persian officials and administrators in the region with his own. This move might have earned him great respect among the Jews, although there is little evidence that they regarded him with any particular affection while under his rule. After his death in 323 BCE, his victories and achievements began to be regarded as legendary, and he was then referred to as "the Great." At this point, the Jews sought to associate themselves with him.

Alexander in the Jewish Tradition

Jewish legends and sources began to develop accounts of a potential visit Alexander might have made to various regions of Yehud Medinata. One of the most well-known accounts is the story of Daniel's vision, which is narrated in the Book of Daniel. In the vision, Daniel sees a ram with two horns, symbolizing the kings of Media and Persia, and a goat coming from the west, which represents Alexander the Great. The goat defeats the ram, indicating the victory of the Greeks over the Persian Empire.

Other stories spawned off of this one, including one that narrates the arrival of Alexander the Great in Jerusalem. In this story, he is greeted by the high priest of Yehud Medinata, who offers his allegiance and submission to Alexander. In return, he entered the Temple and offered a sacrifice, as per Jewish tradition.

This story embeds Alexander the Great in Jewish tradition as a follower of the faith. Not only would his visit to Jerusalem have required him to take a detour on his way to Egypt, but the story also narrates that he bowed down to the high priest upon seeing him in recognition of the greatness of Yahweh. However, no other accounts of such a journey or occurrence have been found outside of the Jewish tradition.

Alexander in Samaria

While the Jews in Yehud Medinata appeared to have welcomed Alexander with reverence, the same was not the case in Samaria. Initially, Alexander had the support of the Samaritan governor, Sanballat III, and was given permission to construct a temple on Mount Gerizim. However, Sanballat III's death led to rebellions in Samaria against Alexander, resulting in rioting and the immolation of the new governor.

Alexander the Great retaliated, leading an army against the Samaritans. He destroyed the city and banished its citizens. The Samaritans exiled themselves to the fount of Mount Gerizim, where they split into two factions. One faction continued living at the foot of the sacred mountain, the city of Samaria, which became a Greek city following their banishment.

Alexander's Legacy

Following Alexander's death in 323 BCE, his vast empire could not maintain peace. His former empire was plunged into civil wars for the next two decades, and when the wars finally ceased, Alexander's once-great empire was divided into distinct sections, the most notable of which belonged to his generals Seleucus and Ptolemy.

The Seleucid Kingdom comprised most of Asia Minor, Mesopotamia, and Syria. The Ptolemaic Kingdom was based in Egypt. During the 3rd century BCE, Judea, which was nestled between the two empires, remained under Ptolemaic rule until the incursion engineered by the Seleucids, at which point it was overseen by the Seleucid Empire for around a century.

While other generals emerged victorious from the civil wars sparked by Alexander the Great's death, the bigger challenge was to legitimize their succession to the throne in the eyes of the local population. The region of the Near East, including Judea and most of the former Persian Empire, had been ruled by a monarchy, with the throne passing from father to son or another male relative. This was not a dynastic law that Alexander's successors could follow since none of his generals were related to him.

One of the ways in which the generals attempted to establish the legitimacy of their rule was to found new Greek cities and name them after themselves, similar to what Alexander had done in conquered lands, with one such example being Alexandria. These cities boasted Greek culture, religion, and art, as well as Greek-style council houses and temples. By doing this, the Greek culture spread among local populations, who appreciated the acclimatization to the Greek way of life and absorbed it into their own, thus leading to a period of Hellenization. Hellenization was a terrific tool the Greek governors used to obtain loyalty among the locals.

Ptolemaic Rule over Judea

While the Greeks kept extensive written records of their history, there is little mention of the region of Judea. Politically, geographically, and socially, this region was of little significance to the Greeks. It did not provide any important trade routes, and entry into Egypt was possible through the coastal plains of Palestine, so the Greeks did not need to go through the mountainous paths of Judea. Since the Jews also had little political involvement, they did not play a significant role in Greek history.

However, the arrival of the Greeks had a great impact on the Jews. This can be observed most noticeably in the coinage system, which changed to reflect the new rule over the region. The weight of the coinage also changed to reflect the Greek Attic weight system. However, within Judea, few political changes took place.

While other surrounding regions like Samaria and Ashdod became hyparchies (administrative units) under the Ptolemaic Empire, with the hipparchs (who managed the administration and governorship of the region) being directly instated by the Ptolemaic ruler, Judea remained relatively independent. It was answerable to the empire but was allowed to operate as a separate administrative unit governed by the high priests. This relative independence kept the peace, and life did not change significantly for the Jews.

The Seleucid Empire

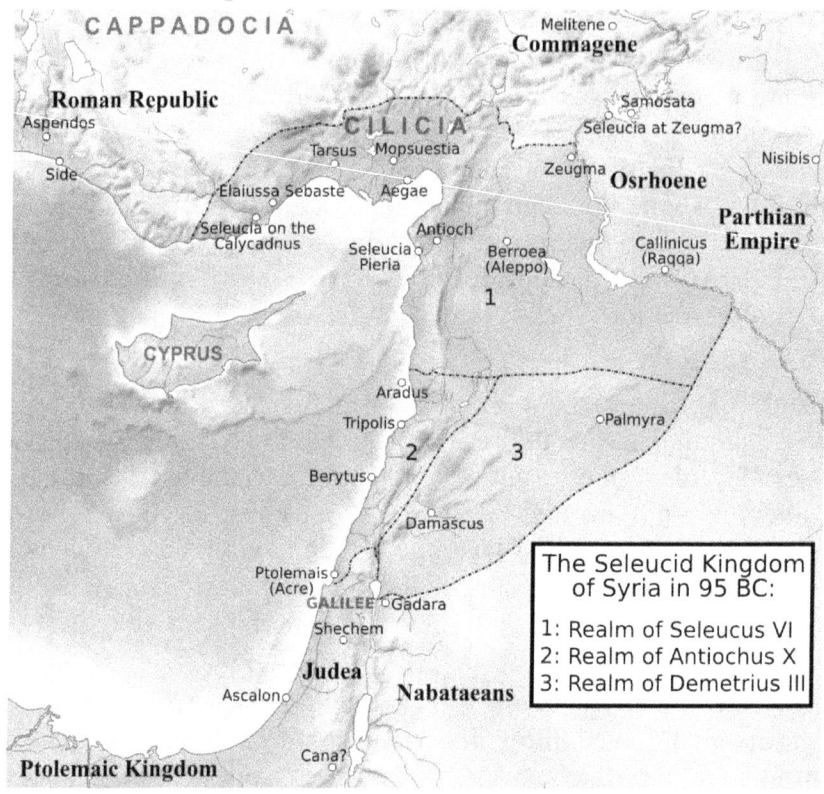

Syria in the Seleucid Empire.
Constantine Plakidas, CC BY-SA 4.0 <https://creativecommons.org/licenses/by-sa/4.0>, via Wikimedia Commons;
https://commons.wikimedia.org/wiki/File:Syria_under_the_Seleucids_95_BC.svg

Seleucus, who was a senior officer in Alexander's army, established his empire in Mesopotamia. Seleucus was not happy governing a small section of the vast Macedonian Empire and engaged in a ruthless expansionist strategy, adding Anatolia, Persia, and the Levant to his territory. Eventually, Judea fell under Seleucid rule a couple of years after Antiochus III won the Battle of Panium in 200 BCE.

Under Antiochus III, Hellenization began, which involved forced conversion to the Greek religion and the practice of Greek culture among local communities. Since embracing the Greek culture brought economic benefits, many Jews accepted Hellenism. However, there were many who did not, and tensions ran high.

Antiochus III's successor, Antiochus IV, implemented a far stricter policy, attempting to convert the entire Jewish population to the Greek religion. He constructed a Greek gymnasium outside the Jewish Temple. He not only required that those who could afford it visit it but also that they remove all clothing before doing so, an act that went against Jewish law. Following a short-lived rebellion, Jewish practices like the Sabbath and circumcision were outlawed, and the worship of Greek gods was made obligatory. Refusing to do so was punishable by death.

The Maccabees, a rebel group, rose up under the leadership of Mattathias, a priest, in 167 BCE. A guerilla war began, with the Jews destroying Greek temples. They met the Seleucid army, and even though they were heavily outnumbered, they inflicted a defeat on the Seleucids and took back Jerusalem. The Jewish people ended the Seleucid rule and instated an autonomous rule.

Hellenistic Impact on the Hasmonean Dynasty

The Hasmonean dynasty emerged as a direct consequence of the Hellenistic influence experienced in Judea. Even during the rule of Alexander the Great and the Ptolemaic rule, the Jews had lived in relative harmony, undisturbed by the shifting hands of the ruling powers. The region had little to offer in the form of economic benefits or political threats.

This political scenery changed drastically with the Seleucid Empire. If the Seleucid Empire had maintained the policies of previous rulers and allowed the Jewish people to have relative autonomy in governance and religion, it is unlikely they would have made any significant contributions to the political climate of the Near East. However, the expansionist policies of Antiochus III and Antiochus IV created much friction, even before outrageous and discriminatory laws were imposed on the Jewish people.

The final straw appeared to be the imposition of the Greek religion on the Jews. The Maccabees rose up against the Seleucids and reinstated Jewish autonomy with the Hasmonean dynasty, which remained independent for over a century. However, Hellenistic influences could not be wholly removed from Judea. It continued to permeate Jewish life as remnants from the way of life in Judea under Seleucid rule. These included changes in the organization of the state and the laws of the land. It even impacted the way art was created and consumed.

Hellenistic Impact on the Herodian Dynasty

The Hasmonean dynasty was followed by the Herodian dynasty, which started under Herod, the Roman-Jewish client king of Judea. Herod the Great inherited a Hellenistic model of kingship, and he attempted to establish a sense of continuity by adopting Hasmonean practices, such as having his coinage minted with Hasmonean symbols and architectural designs. The preexisting Hellenized nature of Judean culture, politics, and social setup influenced Herod's approach to ruling. By using the same system as before, he helped establish legitimacy for his rule. However, following his death, his kingdom was divided into a tetrarchy, which was ruled by his three sons. This rule proved so ineffective that the Romans were forced to interfere in Judea.

Chapter 8: The Hasmonean Dynasty (140–37 BCE)

In 331 BCE, the Achaemenid Empire fell to Alexander the Great, and the period of the Macedonian Empire began, which gave rise to Hellenization in the lands that had been previously under the rule of the Persian Empire. The Greek takeover did not significantly change life in Yehud Medinata, as Persian officials were simply replaced with Greek administrators. Divide and conflict came with the death of Alexander the Great in 323 BCE since his kingdom lay in dispute with no legal heir to claim it.

As such, his generals broke away from the united Macedonian Empire to form their own rule over the lands, and Yehud Medinata lay determinedly in the crosshairs of the Seleucid and Ptolemaic Empires. Caught in a power struggle between the two empires, the Jews were first ruled by the Ptolemies, who gave the Jews relative autonomy, and then by the Seleucids. The Seleucid rule took away Jewish autonomy and exerted greater Hellenistic influence in the region. It also gave rise to the Maccabean Revolt and the Hasmonean dynasty.

The Rise of Jewish Hellenization

The process of Hellenization that began with the arrival of the Seleucids created significant internal conflicts within the Jewish community. Some Jews remained loyal to Ptolemaic rule and did not wish to abandon their traditional values so easily. Others, particularly those who more eagerly accepted the Hellenization process and began to conform to Greek culture, became pro-Seleucid.

This conflict between the Jews even led to a brief civil war in 175 BCE, which pitted High Priest Onias III against his brother Jason, with the latter favoring the Seleucids and Hellenization. The high priest did not. After a period of conflict, bribery, and accusations of murder, Jason was successfully installed as the high priest, and a more widespread Hellenization process began. Onias III was killed by an official named Heliodorus, who was encouraged to do so by Jason.

Jason's accession to the role of high priest might have acted as the final determinant of Jewish Hellenization. Jerusalem became more akin to a Greek city under him, with a gymnasium that Jews would attend for the purpose of nude socialization after undergoing non-surgical restoration of the foreskin. This was to avoid the stigma of circumcision, a practice the Greeks considered barbaric and unacceptable.

Unrest in Judea

The Hellenization of the Jews was not the only reason for the Jewish uprising against the Seleucid rule. Jason's success in establishing himself as high priest and in promoting the Hellenization process, as well as many Jews' eager acceptance of this new culture, indicates that dislike of the Greeks and their culture was not the primary factor.

Antiochus IV's excessive and, at times, barbaric policies toward Jerusalem helped lead to a rebellion. Antiochus had been asked to withdraw from Egypt in 168 BCE by the Romans in the middle of a successful campaign in the region. In his absence, rumors of his death spread among the Jews. Menelaus, Jason's younger brother, was acting as high priest after undermining Jason in front of Antiochus and convincing him to depose Jason. Jason took the news of Antiochus's presumed death as a sign and attacked Jerusalem, driving Menelaus to take refuge in a Seleucid fortress.

Antiochus returned to Judea upon hearing this news. He drove Jason out and proceeded to impose excessive policies on the Jews, presumably to prevent any further actions like what Jason had done. The Jews were required to pay heavy taxes, and their rights to practice their religion were almost completely taken away. Antiochus attempted to suppress all observances of the Jewish religion and customs. He even desecrated the Temple Mount by establishing an idol of Zeus there. The practice of Jewish customs, such as sacrifices, circumcision, and even the Sabbath, was punishable by death. These actions appeared to be the last straw for the Jews, especially those who were already opposed to Hellenization.

The Maccabean Revolt

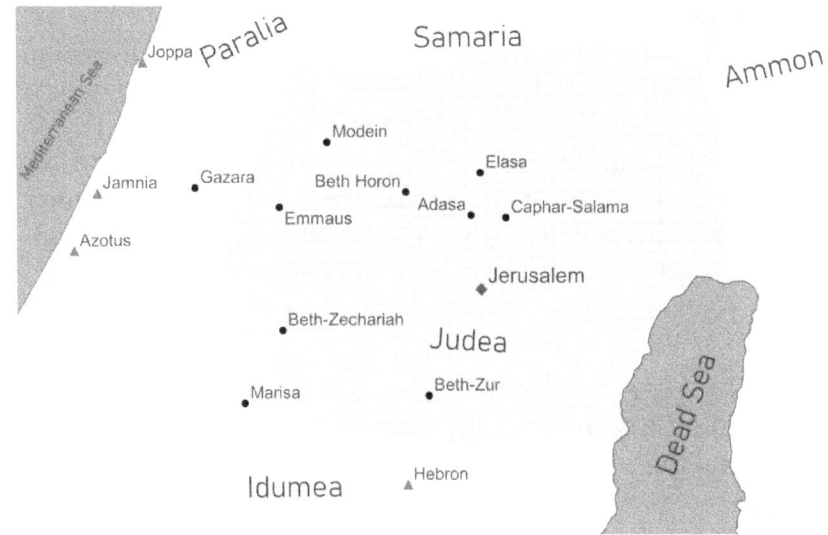

Region of the Maccabean Revolt.
SnowFire, CC BY 4.0 <https://creativecommons.org/licenses/by/4.0>, via Wikimedia Commons; https://commons.wikimedia.org/wiki/File:Judea-Maccabees-Battles.png

The Maccabean Revolt was led by Mattathias, who was part of a priestly family that came to be known as Jewish rebels, the Maccabees, in 167 BCE. The name Maccabee was a title of honor originally given to a son of Mattathias, Judas, in recognition of the role he played in the revolt, and the title was eventually extended to include his whole family. Mattathias encouraged the Jewish people to gather for a holy war against the foreign rulers and began to gather men for a military campaign, which was led by Mattathias's sons Judas, Simon, and Jonathan.

This initial attempt at an uprising was largely unsuccessful and cost the Jews, primarily because the Jews refused to fight or engage in any kind of violence on the Sabbath. It wasn't until one thousand Jewish men, women, and children were killed at the hands of the Seleucids that some Jews reasoned it would be acceptable to fight back. Seven years of warfare ensued, and Judas's guerilla warfare techniques proved successful in securing a victory against the Seleucids.

The Jews had few weapons to speak of; they mainly used modified farm tools in their attacks. Judas's initial tactic was to move slowly and use a hit-and-run approach, lying in ambush for small bands of Seleucid forces. Meanwhile, he slowly increased the number of his own men and added what he had obtained from attacking Seleucid forces to the Jewish arsenal.

Scholars disagree on the immediate causes behind the rise of the Maccabees. It might have been a combination of factors, including the opposition of traditional Jews against the reformists, who had accepted a different culture and religion and abandoned their roots. The First Book of Maccabees cite the Maccabean Revolt as an uprising of Jews against the barbaric Seleucid king who had attempted to eradicate their religion and, therefore, their identity. The Second Book of Maccabees calls the revolt a conflict between Judaism and Hellenization—that is, those who still practiced traditional Jewish values and those who had abandoned them.

Since there is no clear motive behind Antiochus IV's actions in banning the Jewish faith, some historians argue this might have been his attempt to end the conflict between traditional and Hellenized Jews. The rising unrest between traditional and Hellenized Jews could have pushed Antiochus to instate extreme measures to maintain peace in the region, as the practice of banning local religions was rare and against Seleucid tradition. Eventually, both the Hellenization and the actions of the king pushed the traditional Jews to take a stand to gain back their religion and customs.

The Battle of Beth Horon

The Syrians marched with two thousand men in 167 BCE, and Judas's men lay in wait along a narrow pass near Nahal el-Haramiah. Unprepared for the ambush, the Syrian army was completely destroyed, and Seron, a general in Antiochus's army, led the charge against the Jews. Their victory over the Syrian band gave the Jews a much-needed boost in morale and weapons.

In the hopes of avoiding detection and ambushes, the Seleucids took an alternate route to Jerusalem in 166 BCE, which led over wide coastal plains and through the pass at Beth Horon. However, Jewish lookouts saw the approaching Seleucid army and prepared a thousand-man force to meet the Seleucids. Once again, the advancing army was forced into a narrow passage, which Seron dealt with more carefully than the Syrian army had. He had his army proceed through the passage with gaps among individual units, making it impossible to trap the entire army in the event of an ambush.

The Jews, led by Judas, led an attack against the vanguard, immediately killing Seron, with archers simultaneously launching an attack on either side of the Seleucid army. The Seleucids were then attacked from behind by the Jews with the swords they had won from the Syrians. The Seleucids fled, leaving much equipment behind, and were chased back to the coastal plain, where many were killed. Following this victory, the Jewish army grew to more than six thousand in number and came to be reckoned as a formidable force by the Seleucid army.

The Death of Judas

Statue of Judas Maccabeus, Milan.
Yair Haklai, CC BY-SA 4.0 <https://creativecommons.org/licenses/by-sa/4.0>, via Wikimedia Commons; https://commons.wikimedia.org/wiki/File:Statue_of_Judas_Maccabeus_at_exterior_of_the_Duomo_(Milan).j
pg

The Jewish army defeated another Seleucid army under Nicanor at the Battle of Adasa. Following this, a Seleucid army numbering nearly twenty-two thousand men was sent to fight the Jews at the Battle of Elasa. Before the confrontation, Bacchides, who led the Seleucids, marched to Galilee and massacred a large number of Jews and then marched to

Judea, forcing Judas to meet him in open battle.

The two forces met between the plains of Elasa and Berea in an open land that favored the Seleucids, as it was not suited to the Jews' tactics of ambush. The Jews' initial attack made the Seleucids retreat, with the Jews chasing after them. This might have been a purposeful maneuver to draw the Jews into a position where they could be surrounded with no means of retreat. The Seleucids were able to regain their positions and trapped Judas's army. He was killed, and those who survived fled the battle.

Bacchides' victory and the death of Judas reestablished Seleucid authority over the region, and Bacchides went about fortifying major cities. He also took hostages from prominent Jewish families to ensure they would not join the rebellion. Judas was replaced by his brother Jonathan as leader of the Maccabees, though his encounters with the Seleucids did not achieve much.

The Hasmonean Dynasty Is Formed

While the Maccabees rose up in rebellion against the Seleucid Empire, King Demetrius I Soter of the Seleucid Empire, who had taken over for Antiochus IV nearly five years after the beginning of the Maccabean Revolt, was struggling against the Greek king of Pergamon and the king and queen of Egypt, Ptolemy VI and Cleopatra II. The Seleucid king's relations were deteriorating with these rulers so much that they withdrew their support from Demetrius and instead supported Alexander Balas, who laid claim to the throne as the supposed son of Antiochus IV.

This put Demetrius in a difficult position, and he was forced to recall his troops from around Judea to strengthen his forces. In a strategic move, he offered Jonathan lucrative terms to earn his loyalty and diffuse the situation to fortify his position as king. Jonathan moved to Jerusalem in acceptance of these terms in 153 BCE. The terms allowed him to continue building up his army and released hostages in Acre. Once Jonathan was in Jerusalem, he began working on fortifying the city.

Alexander Balas offered Jonathan even better terms, which included appointing him as high priest. Though Demetrius immediately tried to rectify the situation, writing Jonathan a letter that made promises that he could not hope to fulfill, his efforts were in vain. Jonathan accepted Balas's terms and declared allegiance to him. As high priest, Jonathan held an important office, and as a result, so did the Hasmoneans, which protected them from attacks by the Seleucids or supporters of Hellenism. From 153 BCE to 37 BCE, the Hasmoneans held the influential position of high priest in Judea.

The alliance between Balas and Jonathan appeared more than just a strategic move. In 150 BCE, Demetrius lost the throne and was killed by Balas, who became king and married Ptolemy's daughter. Given Jonathan's allegiance to Balas, the former was invited to the ceremony and arrived with many presents, sitting among the kings as an equal. Balas also offered Jonathan royal garments, appointed him *meridarch* (governor), and sent him back to Jerusalem in honor, despite the complaints of the Jewish Hellenists.

The Rule of the Hasmoneans

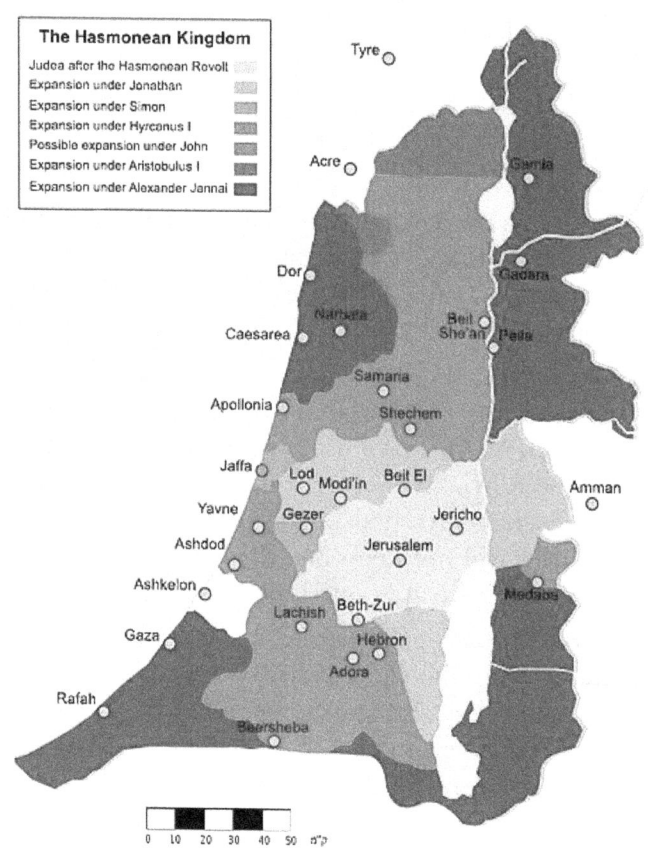

The Hasmonean dynasty.
Effib, CC BY-SA 4.0 <https://creativecommons.org/licenses/by-sa/4.0>, via Wikimedia Commons; https://commons.wikimedia.org/wiki/File:Hasmonean_kingdom.jpg

The beginning of the Hasmonean rule is marked by bids for the throne between various members of the Seleucid Empire, among whom the Hasmoneans often switched allegiances. In 147 BCE, while Demetrius II laid claim to Balas's throne, Jonathan was challenged to a battle by Apollonius, the governor of Coele-Syria. Jonathan and his brother Simon led a force of ten thousand men against Apollonius and attacked the Syrian force unexpectedly in Jaffa, which was forced to surrender quickly. However, Apollonius was not as quick to accept defeat. He gathered reinforcements from the city of Azotus and met Jonathan's army again in the plains. Jonathan was able to capture Azotus and burn the city, along with its temple and the surrounding regions.

Balas honored Jonathan for his victory, but Ptolemy VI, his son-in-law, marched to make war against Balas. Jonathan met Ptolemy VI at Jaffa and forged an alliance, maintaining peace with Egypt, despite their differing support for who should sit on the Seleucid throne. In 145 BCE, Balas was defeated by Ptolemy VI, who himself died in battle, and Demetrius II took the Seleucid throne.

Jonathan adopted a unique approach against the new king, laying siege to the city of Acre, a symbol of Seleucid rule over Judea. When Demetrius II marched to meet Jonathan, Jonathan offered him gifts. An alliance was formed, and the Jews were given an exemption on taxes. Jonathan lifted the siege and returned the city to the Seleucids.

When a new claimant to the throne emerged, the son of Balas, Antiochus VI, under the helpful guidance of a former general of Balas named Diodotus, Demetrius promised to withdraw Seleucid forces from Acre. In return, he officially instated Jonathan as his ally and asked for his aid, which Jonathan provided in the form of three thousand men. However, Demetrius did not keep his word, and Jonathan switched his allegiance to Diodotus, who appointed Simon general of Paralia.

Jonathan and Simon made successful conquests, such as Gaza, Ashkelon, Hazar, and Beth-Zur. Jonathan was also able to form friendly relations with the Romans and the Spartans. However, Jonathan's new alliance with the Seleucid claimant could not be trusted, as Diodotus had no plans to honor the terms of their alliance. Diodotus invited Jonathan to Scythopolis under the guise of a conference, persuading him to dismiss his army of forty thousand men. Not sensing a trap, Jonathan's remaining one thousand men were killed at Ptolemais, and he was taken prisoner by Diodotus in 142 BCE. He was succeeded as high priest by

his brother Simon.
Simon Thassi Becomes High Priest
Simon became the high priest and the prince of Israel, the first to hold this title, following his brother's capture. His army blocked Diodotus's entry into Judea, and Diodotus demanded Jonathan's two sons as hostages in exchange for Jonathan's release. Despite not trusting Diodotus, Simon complied to show the people he had done everything possible to save his brother. However, Diodotus was frustrated by the lack of progress he made in Judea, as Simon's army blocked his passage. He executed Jonathan and kept his sons hostage.

Following Simon's election to office by a priestly assembly, which is narrated in the First Book of Maccabees, his first order of business was to fortify Jerusalem and secure the port of Joppa. Simon then forged an alliance with Demetrius II and asked for tax exemptions for the country, which were granted. Simon is recognized as the first leader of the Hasmonean dynasty since the nation became independent of Seleucid rule under his guidance. The dynasty was declared in the same resolution that declared Simon king of the Hasmoneans, which was adopted in 141 BCE.

For the duration of his kingship, Simon ruled in relative peace. His end came at the hands of his son-in-law Ptolemy, who killed him and his two sons, Judah and Mattathias, at a banquet. Simon was succeeded by his remaining son, John Hyrcanus, in 135 BCE. However, he was unable to avenge his father and brothers.

John Hyrcanus
The sudden death of John Hyrcanus's father and brothers created a precarious political situation. Antiochus VII, who succeeded Demetrius following the latter's capture by the Parthians, entered Judea and laid siege to Jerusalem. The siege stretched on for a year, and Hyrcanus's attempts to evacuate the people who could not fight were in vain, as they were unable to pass through Antiochus's army. Finally, when food supplies began to run short, Hyrcanus negotiated peace with Antiochus.

The truce between the two parties required tribute to be paid to Antiochus, the Jews' aid in the Seleucid campaign against the Parthians, and the unequivocal acceptance of Seleucid rule. Under the rule of Hyrcanus, the Hasmonean dynasty faced immense struggles but also one of the greatest periods of its rule, given the expansion of the dynasty to Idumea (Edom) and Samaria. Under the Seleucids, the Hasmonean dynasty and the Jews under its rule struggled economically, a situation made worse by the high taxes levied on them by Antiochus VII.

In addition, Hyrcanus lost much support and became the reason for dissatisfaction and unrest among the population. Since he was forced to aid Antiochus's military campaigns, he was an absent ruler. His raid of the Tomb of David to pay tribute to Antiochus to end his siege of Jerusalem and his attempt to drive out the civilians of Jerusalem during the siege did not earn him any favors. It was not until Antiochus's death in 129 BCE that Hyrcanus emerged as a powerful leader.

Hyrcanus took advantage of the unrest in the Seleucid Empire and gathered a mercenary force, declaring Judea an independent state. By the time Demetrius II returned from exile in 130 BCE to take control of his empire once again, the power dynamic had shifted too greatly for him to make much headway.

Following Antiochus VII's death in 129 BCE, a period of unrest began in the Seleucid Empire. His death resulted in a victory for the Parthians, ending Seleucid rule over them. In 116 BCE, Antiochus VIII and Antiochus XI, who were half-brothers of Antiochus VII, broke out in a civil war, leading to the further disintegration of the empire.

In 113 BCE, Hyrcanus began extensive military operations. He was able to take Samaria after a difficult year-long siege, with the Samaritans being aided by Antiochus VIII.

Hyrcanus also invaded Transjordan in 110 BCE and laid a six-month siege to Medeba, after which he moved on to Mount Gerizim and Shechem. He was also able to conquer the Edomite towns of Maresha and Adora, among others. With every conquest, Hyrcanus forced the non-Jewish population to accept and observe Jewish customs, a first for any Hasmonean ruler. Before he died, he called for a separation of the office of civil authority between the offices of the king and high priest. He appointed his wife as the civil administrator and his son, Judah Aristobulus, as high priest. He died in 104 BCE, leaving the Hasmonean dynasty to his wife and son.

Alexander Jannaeus

Aristobulus rightfully came into the office of high priest but did not approve of his father's decision to split authority. So, he imprisoned his mother and three brothers and took on the title of king. During his short-lived rule, he was able to conquer Galilee, but he died of an illness in 103 BCE after having ruled for hardly a year. His widow released his brothers from prison; his mother had died of starvation before Aristobulus's death. One of the brothers, Alexander Jannaeus, took the throne.

Hyrcanus's reign was marked by successful expansion, and Alexander Jannaeus adopted much the same approach; however, his rule is regarded as much more violent and stuck in a never-ending cycle of conflict. Alexander began his rule with an attack on Ptolemais at the same time Zoilus of the city of Dora attempted to take the city. Zoilus was defeated by the Hasmoneans. The city of Ptolemais requested the aid of Ptolemy IX before realizing this would unintentionally declare war against Ptolemy's mother, Cleopatra III, who had banished her son. Alexander did not wish to become trapped in a civil war, so he abandoned the campaign. Instead, he secretly forged an alliance with Cleopatra and then offered Ptolemy tribute so he could continue his campaign without direct involvement.

After learning of Alexander's betrayal, Ptolemy laid siege to Ptolemais and pursued Alexander, destroying much of Galilee in the process. At the Battle of Asophon, Alexander's armies were defeated by Ptolemy, who had amassed a formidable force and went on to conquer much of the regions ruled by the Hasmonean dynasty. It wasn't until Cleopatra interfered that Ptolemy withdrew to Cyprus. Alexander bowed before Cleopatra, and she allowed him to retain his rule.

Alexander's successes could not satisfy the Jews at home. The Judean civil war was primarily invoked during an incident at the Feast of Tabernacles, which Alexander presided over as high priest. During the libation ceremony, he threw water over his feet rather than pouring it over the altar, a move that upset the Pharisees. The Pharisees were a group that strictly followed traditional laws and customs. Alexander's display of frustration against the Pharisees earned him the wrath of the people, who began to insult and throw citrons at him. In response, he killed some six thousand Jews and built wooden barriers around the altar to prevent people from coming near him.

While Alexander was at first victorious in the civil conflicts that started around 92 BCE, he began to struggle when the Jews sought the aid of the Seleucids. Demetrius III provided aid and defeated Alexander at Shechem, where he was forced to withdraw into the mountains. In sympathy, around six thousand rebel Jews returned to Alexander, and he launched further attacks until Demetrius was forced to withdraw.

Alexander was able to quash the rebellion and had about eight hundred Jews executed after they were forced to watch their wives and children be executed.

Alexander's reign continued, expanding the Hasmonean Kingdom into Gaulanitis and Galaaditis, as well as Transjordan. He died of an illness caused by a combination of alcoholism and malaria. He died in 76 BCE and was succeeded by his wife, Alexandra. Their son, Hyrcanus II, was named high priest.

Hyrcanus II

Alexandra was the only Jewish queen in the era of the Second Temple (the era of Jewish autonomy after the end of the Babylonian exile), and she named Hyrcanus II her successor, a role he took over after his mother's death in 67 BCE. Within three months of his ascension, Hyrcanus II's rule was challenged by his brother, Aristobulus II. The two met with their forces near Jericho, where many men abandoned Hyrcanus to join Aristobulus, giving him the victory. Hyrcanus fled to Jerusalem and sought refuge in the Second Temple, which was then besieged by his brother. A truce was reached. Hyrcanus had to relinquish the office he held, but he could continue receiving revenue.

However, the truce could not last. Hyrcanus feared his brother would kill him, a fear that was encouraged by Antipater, the general and satrap of Idumea and father to Herod the Great. Antipater wished to control the region through Hyrcanus. Bribed by Antipater, the Nabataeans offered Hyrcanus sanctuary and took Jerusalem, besieging the Temple where Aristobulus had taken refuge. At the same time, Pompey of the Roman Empire had been gaining power after defeating the Seleucids. Since the Romans had been allies of the Hasmoneans since the rule of Judas, both Hyrcanus and Aristobulus asked for aid through Pompey's deputy, Scaurus, who chose to help Aristobulus.

The matter was brought before Pompey, who favored Hyrcanus and chose to help him. Aristobulus then fortified himself in the Temple of Alexandria but surrendered when Pompey's army approached. However, his followers did not, forcing Pompey to lay siege and destroy much of the city and the Temple in the process. Hyrcanus was restored to the office of the high priest, but political authority lay with the Romans. In effect, the actual power lay with Antipater, to whom Hyrcanus deferred all matters.

In 40 BCE, at the instigation of Antigonus, Aristobulus's son, Hyrcanus, was captured by the Parthians. His ears were mutilated, making him ineligible for the high priesthood, thus taking care of the threat he posed. He was then taken to Babylonia, where he lived among the Babylonian Jews. In 36 BCE, Herod I, son of Antipater, defeated Antigonus and had Hyrcanus return to Judea, as he feared that Hyrcanus might encourage the Parthians to fight for the throne alongside him. Six years later, Herod had Hyrcanus executed under the charge of treachery. This was the end of the Hasmonean dynasty, and Herod began the Roman Herodian dynasty.

Chapter 9: The Herodian Dynasty (37 BCE–100 CE)

The foundation of the Herodian dynasty began with Antipater, who exerted great influence over Hyrcanus II and attempted to establish him on the throne as his puppet king. Antipater was able to establish better relations with the Romans, which placed him in a favorable position after Pompey ended Aristobulus's last stand in Jerusalem and established Judea as a Roman vassal state.

Julius Caesar of Rome had initially supported Aristobulus in the Hasmonean conflict, deeming him the stronger of the two candidates. Aristobulus ended up a prisoner in Rome, and Caesar could have used him to take control of Judea were it not for a clever move from Antipater, who was able to secure the favor of Caesar and ensure that Hasmonean rule belonged to Hyrcanus. It was because of Antipater that his sons were able to establish the Herodian dynasty.

Antipater and the Romans

Around 50 BCE, it appeared that Caesar might attempt to use Aristobulus to regain control of Judea. This did not work for Pompey, who had forged an alliance with Antipater and Hyrcanus. Therefore, his supporters had Aristobulus poisoned. Tensions had already been building up from Caesar's ten-year invasion of Gaul. And eventually, those tensions sparked a civil war between Pompey and Caesar. Initially, Hyrcanus, at Antipater's urging, led a force to aid Pompey. When Pompey was murdered in 48 BCE, Antipater turned the Jewish forces to help Caesar.

The Judeans were rewarded for their aid since the Romans lifted their tax obligations. Hyrcanus was reinstated as the ethnarch, or governor, though that position held little actual power, and Antipater ruled over Palestine in 47 BCE. Antipater was also appointed as the Roman procurator, an imperial governor, of Judea. As a result, Antipater was able to further his own cause, appointing his sons to positions of power. After Antipater's assassination in 43 BCE at the hands of the Nabatean king, his sons were able to maintain control of Judea and its puppet king Hyrcanus.

Rise of the Herodians: Herod the Great

Herod the Great.
https://commons.wikimedia.org/wiki/File:HerodtheGreat2.jpg

Herod the Great, son of Antipater, held much of his initial power and influence because of his father. He was made provincial governor of Galilee in 47 BCE, where he managed the taxation system and resolved the region's corruption. In this position, he cultivated a close relationship with the governor of Syria, Sextus Caesar, cousin to Julius Caesar, which secured him the position of general of Coele-Syria. In 41 BCE, Mark Antony, a Roman leader, appointed Herod and his brother Phasael as tetrarchs to serve under Hyrcanus II.

When Antigonus, son of Aristobulus, forcibly took the throne from Hyrcanus in 40 BCE, Herod escaped to Rome and begged the Romans to take a stand against Antigonus and reinstate Hyrcanus. While there, he was unexpectedly named king of the Jews by the Romans and received their aid to help him defeat Antigonus. Herod returned to Judea to win what he saw as his rightful throne from Antigonus. In an attempt to secure his claim to the throne and earn the favor of the Jews, he married Hyrcanus's daughter, Mariamne, banishing his first wife and son in the process.

In 37 BCE, Herod was able to establish himself as the sole ruler of Judea. He led an army and captured Jerusalem, taking Antigonus prisoner and sending him to Mark Antony for execution. Herod's rule might not have been welcomed by all since many Judeans were suspicious of his religious practices and did not believe him to be a true Jew. His involvement with and attempts to appease the Romans, along with his hostile behavior toward the Jewish priestly class, made Judeans less than eager to accept him as one of their own.

Judea under Herod

Herod's thirty-three-year rule over Judea helped him establish the Herodian dynasty. In effect, he was a vassal king to the Romans. However, Herod faced threats to his rule immediately after coming to the throne. His mother-in-law, Alexandra of the Hasmonean dynasty, sought to reestablish Hasmonean rule by having Aristobulus III instated as high priest.

To do this, she sought the help of Cleopatra, who was married to Mark Antony and held some influence over him. Though Cleopatra agreed to help, she also encouraged Alexandra to leave Judea with Aristobulus III to meet Antony. Herod ordered the assassination of Aristobulus III when he heard of the plot. He feared the potential meeting between Antony and Aristobulus, worrying that Aristobulus might be granted the position of high priest. Aristobulus III's assassination removed that threat to Herod's power.

A second threat to Herod's rule emerged when a power struggle began in Rome between Antony and Augustus. Herod, as a Roman vassal, was forced to pick sides. He decided to support Antony. However, Antony was defeated in 31 BCE, and Herod feared his support of Antony might result in him losing the throne. As a result, he was forced to convince Augustus of his loyalty. Herod offered the Romans passage to Syria and Egypt, as well as tribute, and Augustus accepted. While Herod was allowed to rule Judea with autonomy, restrictions were placed on his relationships and dealings with other regions.

Much of Herd's rule was punctuated by distrust and his fear of losing the throne, which drove him to take extreme measures against potential opponents and those who could challenge his rule. Many historians suggest that Herod was not a popular ruler and that the Roman support he received was a major factor in helping him maintain power over Judea, which might have otherwise been crippled under the opposition.

Herod is reported to have taken extreme measures to assuage his fears, including deploying secret police whose job was to gather and report the feelings and attitudes of the Judean population. He acted in secret to prevent any opposition to his rule and made use of force to take down opposers and protestors. Herod also had a bodyguard made up of two thousand men, indicating he constantly feared an attack.

In addition, the lack of Jewishness in his lifestyle remained a major point of contention among the populace. He introduced foreign entertainment in Judea, which was seen as an attempt to promote Roman culture over Jewish culture. The Roman taxes the Judeans were required to pay, combined with the lavish spending by Herod, who constantly prepared excessively valuable gifts in fear of losing his popularity or support among the nobility and the Romans, further angered the Judeans.

At the time of Herod's rule, two major sects lived in Judea: the Pharisees and the Sadducees, the latter belonging to the political elite who shared similar views as the Pharisees. Both groups were unhappy with Herod's rule. The Pharisees had cause for complaint because Herod would not listen to them on matters regarding the construction and restoration of the Temple. The Sadducees were dissatisfied with his rule because Herod had handed their responsibilities for priestly duties in the Temple to Babylonian and Alexandrian outsiders. This move had been made to gain support from the Jewish diaspora living outside of Judea but earned him little favor among the Jewish community.

Architectural Achievements

While Herod did not achieve much in his efforts to be a beloved or even liked ruler, much of his rule focused on architectural projects in

Judea. He undertook the reconstruction of the Second Temple, expanding the platform on which it stood to almost twice its original size and fully restoring the structure. He also began a project to expand the Temple Mount in 19 BCE and used the latest underwater construction and hydraulic techniques to build the Caesarea Maritima. His projects also focused on building several fortresses.

However, these construction projects, much like many other administrative decisions made by Herod, served a selfish purpose. For example, the fortresses were primarily built for him and his family to take refuge in case of an attack. Other construction projects, such as those for the Temple, were intended to appease the Jewish population. Herod also built several cities for pagans to gain their support.

While these projects created substantial employment opportunities for the population, they also burdened the Jews. Herod's projects were funded by taxes, adding to the financial cost of the Judeans since they already had to pay Roman taxes. However, Herod is known to have personally provided for his people during times of crises, such as during a famine in 25 BCE.

The End of Herod

Herod's rule was punctuated by a desire to appease the various factions who were stakeholders in his rule, including the Jews, the non-Jews, and the Romans. As such, his religious policies were designed to cater to all three groups, which produced mixed results in terms of his popularity. His lavish spending was a matter of contention to his Jewish and non-Jewish subjects alike since it added a great financial burden on them. On the other hand, projects like the expansion of the Second Temple might have gained him some favor from the Jews.

Since Herod was proclaimed to be the ruler of all of the Judeans, Jews or otherwise, his policies also catered to the non-Jewish population, which might not have been well received by the Jews. His loyalty to Jewish customs and religion was often questioned because of his heritage, his non-religious practices (such as building temples for the non-Jewish populations), and the murder of his own family members, which he had done to neutralize threats to his throne.

However, some evidence suggests that Herod maintained some degree of Jewish practices in his personal life. While he might have often mixed these practices with Roman and non-Jewish traditions, he did observe some Jewish customs, which is indicated by the construction of mikvehs (baths used to achieve purity) in many of his palaces. And his efforts in building pagan cities for the non-Jewish populations should be praised since they mark the actions of a more accepting ruler than many of the later Hasmonean kings.

Herod died sometime between 5 BCE and 1 CE. The exact date of his death is disputed, though most historians agree it happened in 4 BCE. The cause of his death was an unknown and severe illness dubbed "Herod's Evil." Some narratives claim the illness was so painful that Herod attempted to end his life but was stopped by his cousin, while others suggest his attempt was successful. Regardless, the dissatisfaction with Herod's rule sparked protests and unrest after his death, and the Herodian dynasty changed following the passing of its founder.

The Tetrarchy

Before Herod's death, he created a will. He wanted his kingdom to be divided between his sons. Augustus, the Roman emperor, respected his wishes and split the kingdom in three, with a third going to each son. Herod Archelaus became the ethnarch of the regions of Samaria, Judea, and Idumea (also known as Edom). Philip was made tetrarch of the northern and eastern regions of Jordan, and Antipas was given Galilee and Perea. Of the three, Philip might have ruled with the least amount of trouble, while Archelaus faced harder challenges during his rule.

Herod Archelaus

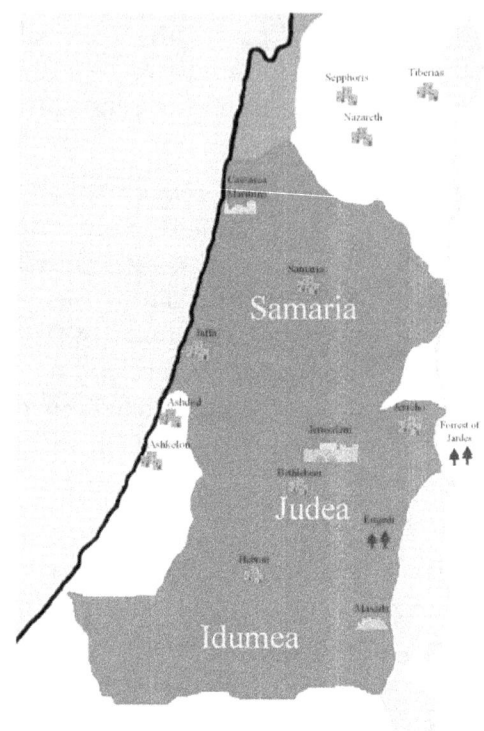

Archelaus's ethnarchy.
Rh0809, CC BY-SA 4.0 <https://creativecommons.org/licenses/by-sa/4.0>, via Wikimedia Commons; https://commons.wikimedia.org/wiki/File:Archelaus_Ethnarchy.jpg

Following his father's illness but before he had officially been declared king or tetrarch, Archelaus attempted to appease the Judean population to secure support for his rule. The protests that had broken out following Herod's death needed to be dealt with immediately to maintain peace in the region. The Judeans demanded lower taxes and the release of political prisoners. Archelaus accepted these terms to show his kindness to the people.

However, the demands of the Judeans did not end there. Herod had erected the statue of a golden eagle over the Temple, which was seen as blasphemous. In the days just before his death, the statue had been cut down, and two teachers and forty students were burned to death as punishment. The people of Judea now demanded punishment for those who had ordered and carried out the immolation of the teachers and youths.

The Jewish population also demanded that the Herod-appointed high priest be deposed and replaced with someone who was more pious. The people's non-stop demands irritated Archelaus, who asked them to be patient and wait for Augustus to officially appoint him king. However, the people did not take kindly to being told to wait, and at night, they began a mourning protest at the Temple for the executed teachers and youths. Archelaus sent several men to ask the mourners to wait until Archelaus had visited Augustus. These soldiers were stoned to death by the mourners, who then returned to their protests.

This incident was the last straw for Archelaus. He ordered the army into the Temple, and a massacre ensued, resulting in the death of some three thousand people. Finding the situation precarious, Archelaus immediately set out for Rome to meet with Augustus, where he was confronted by Antipas, his younger brother. Antipas argued that not only had Archelaus faked his grief for their father's death, but he had also produced a phony will, which gave Archelaus lands that had been intended for Antipas. He also attempted to use the massacre of the three thousand Jews against Archelaus, stating that he had acted inappropriately since he had acted like a king even though he had not yet been appointed as such.

However, the philosopher Nicolaus of Damascus came to Archelaus's aid, stating that he had acted appropriately in his capacity and in accordance with a valid will. The will was verified as having been written by Herod while of sound mind and attested by the keeper of Herod's seal. Whether this was truly the case or if Nicolaus was serving some ulterior motive is unclear. He had been a confidant of Herod during his time, and the keeper of his seal, Ptolemy, was his cousin. After hearing this evidence, Augustus declared Archelaus the ethnarch of Judea, Samaria, and Idumea.

Opposition to Archelaus

Archelaus's rule had many problems from the start. The tensions had begun with the killing of three thousand Jews, but his rule continued to draw ire. For one, it was opposed by his brother, who believed that Archelaus had modified the will and taken the throne that was rightfully his. In addition, Archelaus divorced his first wife, Mariamne III, to marry Glaphyra, the widow of his brother Alexander, even though her second husband was still alive. The marriage went against the Mosaic Law and contributed to Archelaus's rising unpopularity.

Unrest, protests, and general unhappiness and dissatisfaction were rife during Archelaus's rule. As a result, he was unable to manage the lands he was responsible for or the people, as he could not maintain any measure of stability. Complaints of Archelaus's rule reached Augustus, who deposed the former of his rule in 6 CE. Archelaus was exiled to Vienna. The regions of Samaria, Judea, and Idumea became a Roman province. Archelaus never regained his lost throne and died around 18 CE while still in exile.

Philip

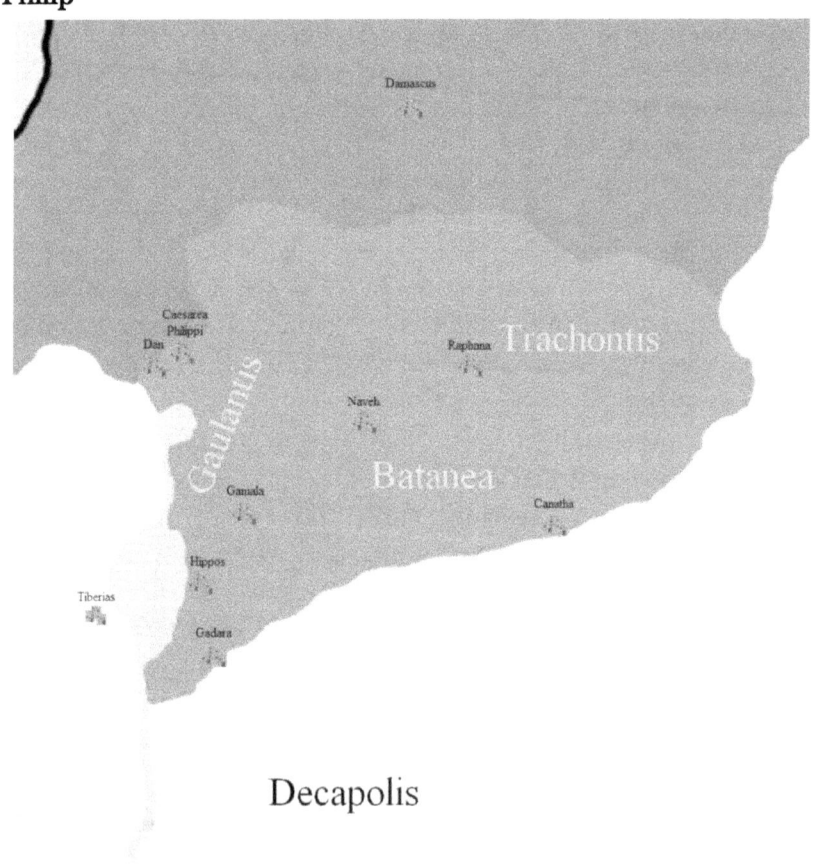

Philip's tetrarchy.
Rh0809, CC BY-SA 4.0 <https://creativecommons.org/licenses/by-sa/4.0>, via Wikimedia Commons; https://commons.wikimedia.org/wiki/File:Herod_Philip_Tetrarchy.png

The second tetrarch of the Herodians was Philip, the half-brother of Antipas and Archelaus. He ruled over regions of Jordan that included Iturea, Trachonitis, Gaulanitis, Paneas, Batanea, and Auranitis. He rebuilt the city of Caesarea Philippa during his rule, which served as the capital of his tetrarchy. Little is known of Philip's reign since most of it was uneventful. Unlike his brothers, Philip ruled in relative peace. He had few Jewish subjects to speak of, so he did not impose any significant Jewish practices on his subjects.

His ruling policy leaned more toward Hellenization. He founded the towns of Bethsaida and another along the Jordan River, which were given large degrees of self-governance in accordance with Roman practice. He was also less extravagant in his rule than his brothers, avoiding long trips to Rome and instead devoting time to his subjects and the tetrarchy. Philip ruled until his death in 34 CE.

Herod Antipas

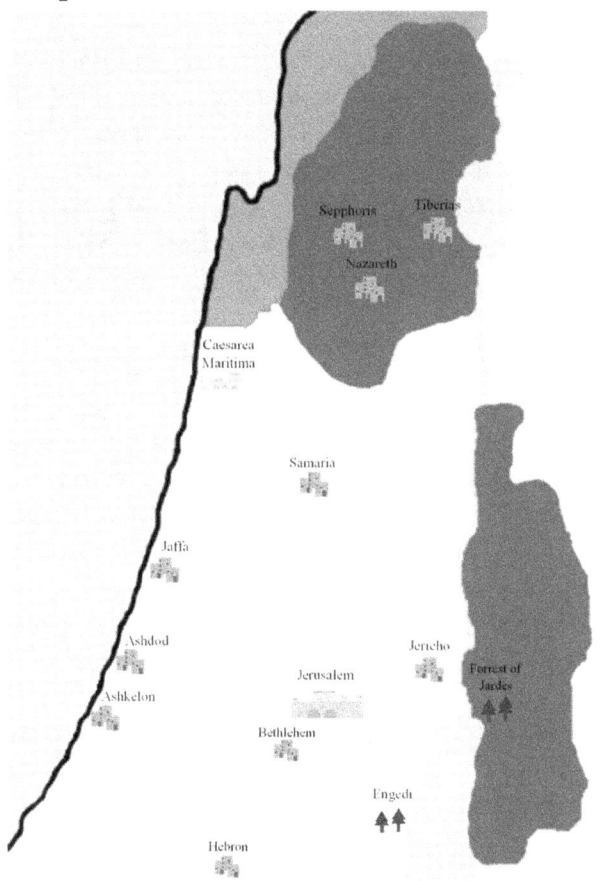

Antipas's tetrarchy.
Rh0809, CC BY-SA 4.0 <https://creativecommons.org/licenses/by-sa/4.0>, via Wikimedia Commons; https://commons.wikimedia.org/wiki/File:Antipas_Tetrarchy.jpg

While Herod Antipas laid claim to the territory that had gone to Archelaus, he was later recognized as a tetrarch by his brother and Augustus, who gave him Galilee and Perea to rule. Antipas had originally argued he should inherit the whole of Judea and rule it as its only king; however, Augustus decided to honor Herod's will. Antipas became ruler of his designated regions in 4 BCE and was immediately faced with unrest.

Just before Antipas assumed office, Judas, son of Hezekiah, attacked the palace at Sepphoris in Galilee, wreaking havoc in the region by looting it and threatening its people. In response, the governor of Syria led an attack in which Sepphoris was destroyed and the inhabitants were enslaved. The borders of Perea were home to constant skirmishes since they connected with the borders of Nabatea.

Antipas's attempts to restore order to these regions included financing construction works. He rebuilt Sepphoris and walled the city of Betharamphtha. He also built his capital city, Tiberias, to the west of the Galilee Sea in honor of Tiberius, who succeeded Augustus in 14 CE. The city held a stadium and a prayer sanctuary and played a significant role as a center of learning during the Jewish-Roman Wars. It was not a successful project at first, as Jews refused to live in it since it was built over a graveyard. Antipas was forced to populate it with forced migrants and slaves.

Contention with John the Baptist

Antipas's conflict with John the Baptist, a Judean prophet and missionary, began over Antipas's marriage. Antipas had been married to the daughter of King Aretas of Nabatea, probably as a strategic move to improve relations between the Nabateans and the Romans. While Antipas was visiting his half-brother, Herod II, he fell for his wife, Herodias, and the two agreed to marry after Antipas divorced his wife. His former wife chose to return to her father, and after having her safely in his custody, Aretas declared war, which might have occurred sometime around 36 CE, two years after Herodias and Antipas were married.

Antipas also faced opposition at home. John the Baptist began preaching between 28 and 29 CE near the Jordan River on the edge of Perea. As related in the Gospel of Mark, he used Antipas's marriage to criticize an incestuous practice, as Herodias was also Antipas's niece and had been his brother's wife. John also encouraged the widespread belief that the two had married while Herodias's first husband still lived, although the two were divorced before her second marriage. Given John's influence, Antipas feared a rebellion since many Jews did not approve of his union with his second wife. John was arrested and imprisoned in the fortress of Machaerus and was executed when Herodias urged her daughter to ask for John's head.

The Execution of Jesus of Nazareth

When Jesus of Nazareth began preaching in Galilee, Antipas feared it was John risen from the dead. Fearful of what might happen, Antipas plotted the execution of Jesus. Jesus was reportedly warned of such a plot and declared that he, as a prophet, was not vulnerable to such schemes. Antipas might have also played a role in his trial. Pontius Pilate, the governor of Judea who presided over the trial of Jesus, sent him to Antipas since Jesus was from Galilee and, therefore, under Antipas's jurisdiction.

Antipas hoped to see Jesus perform a miracle, for which he was known, and was reportedly pleased to see him. But Jesus refused to perform one. Antipas mocked him and sent him back to Pilate, where he was crucified on the charge of blasphemy. Pilate's actions served to improve relations between the two rulers, as Jesus had posed a threat to Antipas's rule and had caused much unrest, thus pacifying the earlier enmity between Pilate and Antipas. It is not known why the two were upset with each other, but many historians believe it may have had something to do with the massacre of some Galileans.

End of Antipas

The hostilities with the Nabatean king turned into an all-out war in 36 CE. After suffering humiliating defeats at the hands of the Nabateans, who were joined by deserters from Antipas's brother, Philip's, armies, Antipas turned to Roman Emperor Tiberius for help. Tiberius ordered the governor of Syria, Vitellius, to provide aid. Vitellius prepared two forces, which were instructed to march around Judea while he attended a festival in Jerusalem, where Antipas was also in attendance. There, news reached Vitellius of Tiberius's death. He stated he no longer held the authority to carry out the attack and recalled his troops, although some sources suggest that an argument between Vitellius and Antipas caused the former to use Tiberius's death as an excuse to withdraw his support.

Antipas's end came at the hands of his nephew, Agrippa, who had turned to his uncle for help when he found himself struggling with much debt. Antipas refused to provide any money. Agrippa was later imprisoned when he was heard telling his friend Caligula that he could not wait for Tiberius to die and for Caligula, Augustus's great-grandson, to become ruler. After Caligula became emperor in 37 CE, he had Agrippa released and gave him Philip's tetrarchy following his death.

Agrippa then set about seeking his revenge and accused Antipas of plotting against the emperor and of stocking up weaponry to lead an assault. Since Antipas had a store of weapons that he could not deny, Caligula believed Agrippa's other accusations and exiled Antipas to an undetermined location, where he died.

The End of the Herodian Dynasty

Agrippa's close friendship with Caligula secured him the position of tetrarch, and he was given Philip's territories in 37 CE. In 40 CE, after Antipas had been exiled, his territories were given to Agrippa. In the following year, Agrippa was also given the territories that had once been governed by Archelaus. Thus, Agrippa reunited the Herodian dynasty as it had once existed under Herod I and became its sole ruler under the Romans.

Agrippa died in 44 CE and was succeeded by his son, Agrippa II. He did not inherit all of his father's territories, nor was he given a rule anywhere as vast as Agrippa I. Instead, he was given the tetrarchy of Chalcis, to which were later added the territories that had once been ruled by Philip. When the first revolt began in the Jewish-Roman Wars, which broke out in response to Roman oppression, heavy taxation, and religious conflicts between the Romans and the Jews, Agrippa II was an active participant on the side of the Romans.

Agrippa had initially attempted to avoid a war with Rome altogether. The Jews refused to pay taxes that were owed to the Romans, and Agrippa desperately tried to pacify the situation by encouraging the people to withstand some of the injustices and accept Roman rule. He failed to suppress the rebellion and was driven out of Jerusalem, along with his sister, Bernice, in 66 CE. He also provided aid to the Roman forces in the form of archers and cavalry units to show his support to the emperor. He even accompanied the Romans on some campaigns. After the capture of Jerusalem, Agrippa II returned to Rome, where he was designated praetor and given additional territories to rule.

With the death of Agrippa II, sometime between 92 and 100 CE, the Herodian dynasty came to an end. The lands ruled by Agrippa as a tetrarch were incorporated into the Roman Empire.

Conclusion

The role ancient Israel played in the formation of religious history and in the current religious landscape cannot be doubted. In the present day, many of the currently practiced religions find their bases in ancient Israel, making its study vital to understand the ways in which these ancient peoples and regions continue to affect modern life.

To begin with, the ancient Israelites introduced one of the world's first monotheistic religions. Before this, most religious practices were polytheistic or, at best, henotheistic, such as during the rule of the Persian Empire. Idol worshiping and the worship of multiple gods and deities were common, and the concept of worshiping a single god was new and unprecedented at the time.

The basis of the Israelite religion, the Ten Commandments, played an important role in the foundations of other religions. The Hebrew scriptures lay the basis of Judaism. The appointment of the Israelites as God's chosen people at Mount Sinai forms an integral part of the Jewish belief system, with Jews having to set an example to the world of righteous behavior.

Moreover, the Israelite religion forms the basis of Christianity, with the Hebrew scriptures forming part of the Old Testament. Christianity also recognizes many prominent Israelite figures, such as David and Abraham. The religion of Islam also recognizes the prophethood of these figures and acknowledges Hebrew scriptures as divine revelations. So, two of the world's largest and most widely practiced religions are derived from Judaism, which itself is an extension of the religion of the ancient Israelites.

Ancient Israelite history began with the Iron Age, and archaeological discoveries have attested to the period with the findings of iron tools in the region. Given that the Bible and the Hebrew scriptures provide an extensive history of the region, archaeological efforts have been focused on making discoveries that can verify or further expand on events related to the Bible. However, in most instances, the religious scriptures offer the only evidence of some events.

The main focus of archaeologists in Israel has always been to explain, expand, or illustrate religious passages through discoveries. Such evidence aids in the interpretation of the Bible. For example, many historians once believed that Jesus might not have been real. Today, enough evidence has been uncovered to attest that he did exist. Thus, it stands to reason that events without significant archaeological evidence might have at least some basis in fact.

The influence of the Israelites persists today in more ways than one. The history of the region, as it transformed from an independent state to being ruled by foreigners to then being granted relative autonomy under the rule of foreign nations, narrates the progress of a nation that survives to this day, with its religious system intact, despite the enmeshment of different cultures and religions throughout the later parts of its existence.

In addition, the architectural feats of the Jews, even during the period of vassal rule, hold great value today. The remains of the Second Temple, which was destroyed by the Romans (only the western wall remains), is a sacred site to Jews today and is a reminder of their plight. However, even though the Jews suffered under foreign religious influences and rulers, they persevered and did not allow their beliefs to fail or be lost to time.

Here's another book by Enthralling History that you might like

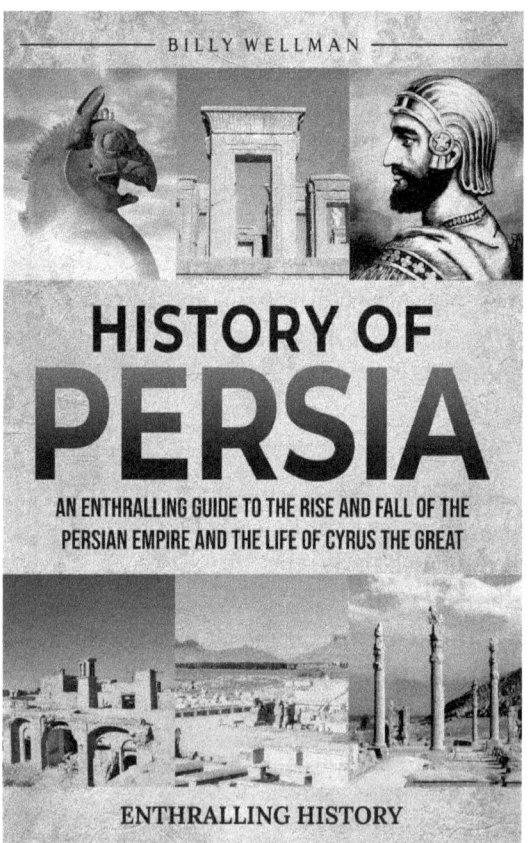

Free limited time bonus

Stop for a moment. We have a free bonus set up for you. The problem is this: we forget 90% of everything that we read after 7 days. Crazy fact, right? Here's the solution: we've created a printable, 1-page pdf summary for this book that you're reading now. All you have to do to get your free pdf summary is to go to the following website:

https://livetolearn.lpages.co/enthrallinghistory/

Once you do, it will be intuitive. Enjoy, and thank you!

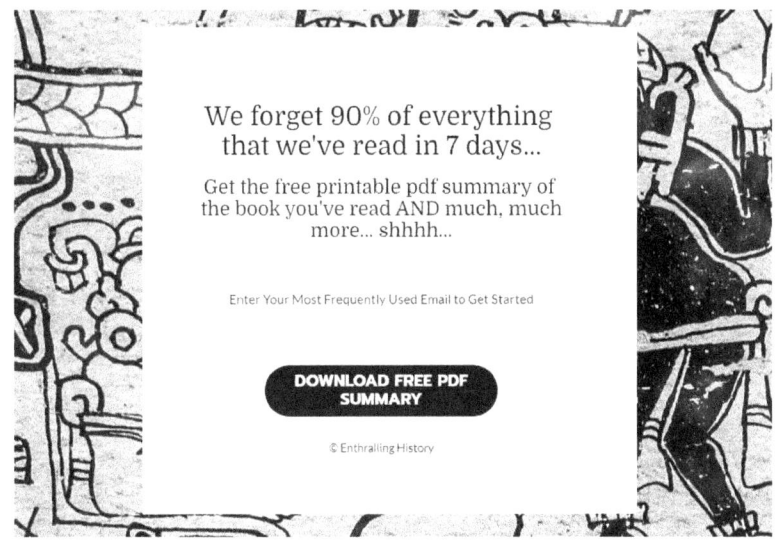

Bibliography

Ballentine, Debra Scoggins. "The Kingdom of Judah." *Bible Odyssey*, 2009, https://www.bibleodyssey.org/places/main-articles/the-kingdom-of-judah/.

Bell, Kelly. "Judas Maccabeus, Hammer of the Jews." *Warfare History Network*, 2009, https://warfarehistorynetwork.com/article/judas-maccabeus-hammer-of-the-jews/.

BibleToday. "WHY IS THE BIBLE GOD'S WORD?" *BibleToday*, 2020, https://www.bibletoday.com/?gclid=Cj0KCQjwt_qgBhDFARIsABcDjOfmwnQ38bDtShSe0SDZZ-3GSLAl-AtwE23EAHE-n1J2Xf0qJkovWdEaAkqZEALw_wcB.

Boston University. "First Temple Period: Jerusalem as the Capital of Judahite Kingdom (930-722)." *Capital of Judah I (930-722)*, 2020, https://www.bu.edu/mzank/Jerusalem/p/period2-2-1.htm.

Britannica, Editors of Encyclopedia. "Biblical literature | Definition, Types, Significance, Survey, & Development." *Encyclopedia Britannica*, 30 March 2023, https://www.britannica.com/topic/biblical-literature.

Britannica, The Editors of Encyclopedia. "Hasmonean dynasty." *Encyclopedia Britannica*, 2021, https://www.britannica.com/topic/Hasmonean-dynasty.

Britannica, The Editors of Encyclopedia. "Israelite." *Encyclopedia Britannica*, 2022, https://www.britannica.com/topic/Israelite.

Britannica, The Editors of Encyclopedia. "Judah | Hebrew tribe | Britannica." *Encyclopedia Britannica*, 2023, https://www.britannica.com/topic/Judah-Hebrew-tribe.

Brown, William. "Ancient Israelite & Judean Religion." *World History Encyclopedia*, 13 July 2017, https://www.worldhistory.org/article/1097/ancient-israelite--judean-religion/.

Cataliotti, Joseph, and Christopher Sailus. "Israelites History, Timeline & Religion | Who were the Israelites? - Video & Lesson Transcript." *Study.com*, 7 October 2022, https://study.com/learn/lesson/israelites-history-timeline-religion-who-were-the-israelites.html.

The Church of Jesus Christ. "The Assyrian Conquest and the Lost Tribes." *The Church of Jesus Christ of Latter-day Saints*, 2022, https://www.churchofjesuschrist.org/study/manual/old-testament-student-manual-kings-malachi/enrichment-d?lang=eng.

Claudia, F. "King Saul of Israel: History & Timeline | Who Was the First King of Israel? - Video & Lesson Transcript." *Study.com*, 21 October 2021, https://study.com/academy/lesson/king-saul-of-israel-history-timeline-quiz.html.

Cornerstone Connections. "The Golden Age of Israel." *Cornerstone Connections*, 2015, https://www.cornerstoneconnections.net/assets/teens/Lessons/2015/Q4/English/TEACHER/CC-15-Q4-L11-T.pdf.

Cundall, Arthur E. "The United Monarchy: Fact or Fiction?" *Vox Evangelica*, vol. 8, 1973, pp. 33-39, https://biblicalstudies.org.uk/pdf/vox/vol08/monarchy_cundall.pdf.

Encyclopedia Judaica. "Antigonus II." *Encyclopedia.com*, 2023, https://www.encyclopedia.com/religion/encyclopedias-almanacs-transcripts-and-maps/antigonus-ii.

Encyclopedia.com. "Hasmoneans." *Encyclopedia.com*, 2018, https://www.encyclopedia.com/people/philosophy-and-religion/judaism-biographies/hasmoneans.

Facts and Details. "MOSES, MT. SINAI, THE TEN COMMANDMENTS, THE GOLDEN CALF AND HIS DEATH JUST SHORT OF THE PROMISED LAND." *Facts and Details*, 2018, https://factsanddetails.com/world/cat55/3sub1/entry-5698.html.

Faust, A. "Cities and Towns in Ancient Israel (Bronze and Iron Ages)." *Encyclopedia of the History of Science, Technology, and Medicine in Non-Western Cultures*, edited by Helaine Selin, Springer, 2008.

Ferguson, John. "Hellenistic age | History, Characteristics, Art, Philosophy, Religion, & Facts." *Encyclopedia Britannica*, 17 March 2023, https://www.britannica.com/event/Hellenistic-Age.

Finkelstein, Israel. "The Campaign of Shoshenq I to Palestine: A Guide to the 10th Century BCE Polity." *eitschrift Des Deutschen Palästina-Vereins*, vol. 118, no. 2, 2002, pp. 109-135. *JSTOR*, https://www.jstor.org/stable/27931693.

Finkelstein, Louis, and W. D. Davies, editors. *The Cambridge History of Judaism: Volume 2, The Hellenistic Age*. Cambridge University Press, 2008.

Fraser, Peter Marshall, et al. "Palestine." *Encyclopedia Britannica*, 21 March 2023, https://www.britannica.com/place/Palestine.

Gier, Nicholas F. "Hebrew Henotheism." *University of Idaho*, 2020, https://www.webpages.uidaho.edu/ngier/henotheism.htm.

Gilad, Elon. "Meet the Hasmoneans: A Brief History of a Violent Epoch - Jewish World." *Haaretz*, 23 December 2014, https://www.haaretz.com/jewish/2014-12-23/ty-article/meet-the-hasmoneans/0000017f-e30d-d75c-a7ff-ff8d7cdd0000.

Gottheil, Richard, and Samuel Krauss. "PTOLEMY I - JewishEncyclopedia.com." *Jewish Encyclopedia*, 2021, https://www.jewishencyclopedia.com/articles/12420-ptolemy-i.

Grabbe, L. L. "The History of Israel: The Persian and Hellenistic Periods." *Text in Context: Essays by Members of the Society for Old Testament Study*, edited by A. D. H. Mayes, OUP Oxford, 2000. Accessed 3 April 2023.

Harris, Raphael. "The Golden Age of Israel." *The Jewish Magazine*, 1999, http://www.jewishmag.com/18mag/golden/golden.htm.

The Hebrew University of Jerusalem. "Hellenistic Period." *Tel Dor*, 2014, http://dor.huji.ac.il/periods_HL.html.

Herron, Dustin. "Israel and Judah: Difference Between the Two Kingdoms." *The Fellowship of Israel Related Ministries*, 2 June 2021, https://firmisrael.org/learn/israel-and-judah-two-kingdoms-and-their-differences/.

Higgins, William. "Dangerous Partnerships: The story of Jehoshaphat & Ahab." *Christian teaching*, 1 March 2008, https://williamshiggins.net/2008/03/01/dangerous-partnerships-the-story-of-jehoshaphat-ahab/.

HISTORY Editors. "Hellenistic Greece." *HISTORY.com*, 4 February 2010, https://www.history.com/topics/ancient-greece/hellenistic-greece.

HISTORY Editors. "Iron Age." *HISTORY*, 3 January 2018, https://www.history.com/topics/pre-history/iron-age.

Horwitz, Aharon. "A Brief History of Ancient Jerusalem | The Jerusalem to do guide - AAJ." *Jerusalem*

Hunt, Robert D. "Herod and Augustus: A Look at Patron-Client Relationships." *BYU ScholarsArchive*, 2002, https://scholarsarchive.byu.edu/cgi/viewcontent.cgi?article=1013&context=studiaantiqua.

Israel Antiquities Authority. "The Archaeological Periods in Israel." *Antiquities.org*, 2022, https://www.antiquities.org.il/t/PeriodSub_en.aspx?id=3.

Israel Embassy. "History: Second Temple." *Israeli Missions Around the World*, 2018, https://embassies.gov.il/baku/AboutIsrael/history/Pages/History-Second-Temple.aspx.

Jarus, Owen. "Ancient Israel: History of the kingdoms and dynasties formed by ancient Jewish people." *Live Science*, 22 September 2022, https://www.livescience.com/55774-ancient-israel.html.

Jewish History. "Alexander the Great." *Jewish History*, 2020, https://www.jewishhistory.org/alexander-the-great/.

King, James, and Frank W. Walbank. "Saul | king of Israel | Britannica." *Encyclopedia Britannica*, 7 March 2023, https://www.britannica.com/biography/Saul-king-of-Israel.

Kunst Historisches Museum Wein. "Judah after Alexander the Great." *Kunst Historisches Museum Wein*, 2020, https://data1.geo.univie.ac.at/projects/muenzeundmacht/showcases/showcase2%3Flanguage=en.html.

Laie, Benjamin T., and Osama Shukir. "Mesopotamian Effects on Israel During the Iron Age." *World History Encyclopedia*, 23 December 2015, https://www.worldhistory.org/article/850/mesopotamian-effects-on-israel-during-the-iron-age/.

Lendering, Jona. "Herod Antipas." *Livius.org*, 4 August 2020, https://www.livius.org/articles/person/herod-antipas/.

Lendering, Jona. "Herod Archelaus." *Livius.org*, 23 April 2020, https://www.livius.org/articles/person/herod-archelaus/.

Lendering, Jona. "Philip." *Livius.org*, 21 April 2020, https://www.livius.org/articles/person/herod-philip/.

Lipschits, Oded, and Manfred Oeming. *Judah and the Judeans in the Persian Period*. Penn State University Press, 2006.

Mark, Joshua J. "Kingdom of Israel." *World History Encyclopedia*, 26 October 2018, https://www.worldhistory.org/Kingdom_of_Israel/.

Maxine Grossman. "Legacy of Ancient Israel - Legacy of Ancient Israel Ancient Israel - "Israel" was first." *University of Maryland*, 2020, https://www.studocu.com/en-us/document/university-of-maryland/introduction-to-the-hebrew-bible/engl262-legacy-of-ancient-israel/40401708.

Miller, Charlotte. "The Importance of the Israelites and Ancient Israel." *LibreTexts*, 2020, https://human.libretexts.org/Bookshelves/History/World_History/Book%3A_World_History_-_Cultures_States_and_Societies_to_1500_(Berger_et_al.)/02%3A_Early_Middle_Eastern_and_Northeast_African_Civilizations/2.12%3A_The_Importance_of_the_Israelites_and_Ancient_Israel

Moulton, Sunday. "Iron Age: Timeline & Facts." *Study.com*, 2023, https://study.com/academy/lesson/iron-age-timeline-facts.html.

Muscato, Christopher. "Kingdom of Judea: History & Explanation - Video & Lesson Transcript." *Study.com*, 2020, https://study.com/academy/lesson/kingdom-of-judea-history-lesson-quiz.html.

Nenner, Ravit, and Noa Evron. "Ancient Jerusalem: The Village, the Town, the City." *Biblical Archaeology Society*, 2022, https://www.biblicalarchaeology.org/daily/biblical-sites-places/jerusalem/ancient-jerusalem/.

New World Encyclopedia. "Henotheism." *New World Encyclopedia*, 2021, https://www.newworldencyclopedia.org/entry/Henotheism.

New World Encyclopedia. "Kingdom of Judah." *New World Encyclopedia*, 2018, https://www.newworldencyclopedia.org/entry/Kingdom_of_Judah.

Oates, Harry. "The Maccabean Revolt." *World History Encyclopedia*, 29 October 2015, https://www.worldhistory.org/article/827/the-maccabean-revolt/.

O'Connor, David, and Stephen Quirke. "Why Were the Philistines and Israelites Enemies." *DailyHistory.org*, 2018, https://dailyhistory.org/Why_Were_the_Philistines_and_Israelites_Enemies.

Penn Museum. "IRON AGE I - Canaan & Ancient Israel @ University of Pennsylvania Museum of Archaeology and Anthropology." *Penn Museum*, 2016, https://www.penn.museum/sites/Canaan/IronAgeI.html.

Prabhat, S. "Israel and Judah." *Difference Between*, 2021, http://www.differencebetween.net/miscellaneous/culture-miscellaneous/difference-between-israel-and-judah/.

Profilbaru. "Yehud (Babylonian province)." *PROFILBARU.COM*, 2023, https://profilbaru.com/article/Yehud_(Babylonian_province).

Rice, Damien, and Matt Galbraith. "Biblical Israel: The Land of Kush." *The Curse of Ham*, Princeton University Press, 2003, https://www.degruyter.com/document/doi/10.1515/9781400828548.17/pdf.

Rice, Damien, and Matt Galbraith. "The Persian Period and the Origins of Israel: Beyond the "Myths."" *Critical Issues in Early Israelite History*, 16 November 2008, https://www.degruyter.com/document/doi/10.1515/9781575065984-007/html.

Ritenbaugh, Richard T. "What the Bible says about Israel's Golden Age." *Bible Tools*, 2013, https://www.bibletools.org/index.cfm/fuseaction/Topical.show/RTD/cgg/ID/17709/Israels-Golden-Age.htm.

Rogerson, J. W. "Israel to the End of the Persian Period: History, Social, Political, and Economic background." *The Oxford Handbook of Biblical Studies*, edited by Judith M. Lieu and J. W. Rogerson, OUP Oxford, 2008.

Rolling, C. "Henotheism in the Bible - 807 Words | 123 Help Me." *123HelpMe.com*, 2020, https://www.123helpme.com/essay/Henotheism-In-The-Bible-526821.

Rooke, Deborah W. *Zadok's Heirs: The Role and Development of the High Priesthood in Ancient Israel*. Clarendon Press, 2000.

Rose, Jenny. "The "Persian" Period - Biblical Studies." *Oxford Bibliographies*, 2020, https://www.oxfordbibliographies.com/display/document/obo-9780195393361/obo-9780195393361-0194.xml.

Ross, Lesli Koppelman. "The Hasmonean Dynasty." *My Jewish Learning*, 2015, https://www.myjewishlearning.com/article/the-hasmonean-dynasty/.

Rubel, Ahsan, and JE Wright. "The Campaign of Pharaoh Shoshenq I in Palestine | Bible Interp." *Bible Interpretation*, 2004, https://bibleinterp.arizona.edu/articles/Wilson-Campaign_of_Shoshenq_I_1.

Schäfer, Peter. "History of the Ptolemies." *Boston University*, 2009, https://www.bu.edu/mzank/Jerusalem/cp/ptolemies.htm.

Shapira, Dan. "Who Were the Hasmoneans?" *Tablet Magazine*, 30 November 2021, https://www.tabletmag.com/sections/history/articles/who-were-the-hasmoneans.

Thomas, Brian C. "Significance of Israel in Bible Prophecy." *God 1st Bible Fellowship*, 2020, https://www.god1st.org/Signficance-of-Israel-in-Prophecy.

TimeMaps. "Ancient Israel: Religion, Culture and History." *TimeMaps*, 2011, https://timemaps.com/civilizations/ancient-israel/.

Trentin, Summer, and Debby Sneed. "The Hellenistic Period-Cultural & Historical Overview | Department of Classics." *University of Colorado Boulder*, 14 June 2018, https://www.colorado.edu/classics/2018/06/14/hellenistic-period-cultural-historical-overview.

United Church of God. "Israel's Golden Age." *United Church of God*, 16 February 2011, https://www.ucg.org/bible-study-tools/booklets/the-united-states-and-britain-in-bible-prophecy/israels-golden-age.

United Church of God. "Israel's Golden Age." *United Church of God*, 16 February 2011, https://www.ucg.org/bible-study-tools/booklets/the-united-states-and-britain-in-bible-prophecy/israels-golden-age.

Velázquez, Efraín, and JE Wright. "The Persian Period and the Origins of Israel: Beyond the "Myths" | Bible Interp." *Bible Interpretation*, 2009, https://bibleinterp.arizona.edu/articles/persian.

World History. "The legacy of ancient Israel." *World history*, 3 September 2015, https://www.worldhistory.biz/ancient-history/70552-the-legacy-of-ancient-israel.html.

Zhakevich, Philip, and Ben Noonan. "From Texts to Scribes: Evidence for Writing in Ancient Israel." *American Society of Overseas Research (ASOR)*, 2021, https://www.asor.org/anetoday/2021/08/writing-in-ancient-israel.